I HOPE YOU WILL ENJOY
MY BOOK. GOD BLESS YOU!

GEORGE JEU

My Journey

To the Past and Back

趙 文 美

到 我
近 的
及 旅
回 程

by George Jeu

HONG KONG
15 JAN 1950
DEPARTED
IMMIGRATION

SEAL OF THE CITY AND COUNTY OF SAN FRANCISCO

PASSPORT CONTROL
HONG KONG
PERMITTED TO LAND
16 JUL 1948
IMMIGRATION OFFICER

PASSPORT

About the Author
George Jeu

George Jeu was born in Memphis, TN on September 23, 1935. He spent his childhood years growing up in Little Rock, AR, Memphis, TN and Long Tin Lay Village in Guangdong Province, Sun Woi District in China.

George experienced many life changing events when he left America as a young boy to live with his Grandfather and Mother in China. These trying times from his childhood made him the man he is today.

For many years, George enjoyed a drafting career working for various architectural firms in the Memphis area such as George A. Thomason and Associates and Bologna and Associates. He also worked as a freelance artist painting signs for Danver's, Shoney's, The Hungry Fisherman and other independent contractors to supplement the family income.

George married Libby on May 4, 1957 and had three daughters: Sherry, Kerri and Anita. They also raised one of George's nephews, Ronald (Ron). The family resided in Memphis until the kids grew up and all moved away. Now George and Libby have both semi-retired and currently reside in Olive Branch, Mississippi.

After moving to Olive Branch, George decided to join a Genealogy class at the Olive Branch Public Library. The first day of class he realized he had gone into the wrong room and was actually in a Memoirs class. After the first session, George decided to stay in the class and begin writing his life story which his wife and children had been asking him to do for years. He saw this as the perfect opportunity to pass down his story to his grandchildren and future generations.

This book is dedicated to
my daughters
Sherry, Kerri and Anita
and to my wife of 56 years
Elizabeth Ann (Libby)

A Special dedication
to my brother
Jimmy
who shared this amazing journey with me.
Jimmy passed away on May 25, 2012.

A special thanks to Kerri for her endless efforts
in helping me with the cover design,
typesetting and layout of my book.

太祖御容

TAI CHO, CHIU HONG YIN
THE FOUNDER OF THE SUNG
DYNASTY.
REIGN: 960 TO 976 A.D.

MR. & MRS. WING YING CHIU

Wing Ying Chiu, author of the book,
"A Brief history of the Chius" 趙

Preface

A surprising revelation from the book *A Brief History of the Chius* (趙), by Wing Ying Chiu. This book was given to me by an elder of the Long Kong Tin Yee Association on Vance Avenue in Memphis, TN. Note: the surname Chiu has one Chinese character that is written like this: 趙 , but it has many English translations and spellings, one of which is "Jeu." This is the English spelling that our family has always used but the Chinese character is the same.

About 50 years after I received this book, I began writing my memoir. During this period of writing and research, I found this book and started studying it in depth. The book is mostly written in Chinese and in the Chinese format, which is different from our English books, being read from right to left, top to bottom and what we consider the back is the front of the book. At the end of the book, is a brief history of the Chiu Clan written in English. I found the name of our first ancestor that entered the Kwangtung Province. In the book, also mentioned, is the "Lung Tin Li" village in Sun Woi District in the Kwangtung Province. This is the village I lived in with my mother and grandfather. The book continued listing generations of people who moved around and noted that the Chius (Jeus) that settled in Kwangtung Province around 1500 A.D. are all direct descendants of the Royal Family.

This was such a profound discovery for me to fully comprehend at the time, to think that our family lineage actually goes back to the Royal family of the Sung Dynasty. How amazing is that! This discovery has kept me focused and encouraged as I continue to write my memoirs.

Our home in America - Memphis, Tennessee in the 1940's

Our home in China - The Village of Long Tin Lay,
Guangdong Province, Sun Woi District

My Journey

My Journey

Part 1
From Memphis, Tn – to the Past
By George Jeu (Mun May)

The year was 1947. It was early October and we were on board a Greyhound Bus leaving Memphis, TN bound for San Francisco, CA to board a ship to China. Making the trip was our Grandfather Jeu Bing Fun, our Mother Jeu Wong Yet Yee, my younger brother Jimmy (age 11) and me (age 12). The purpose

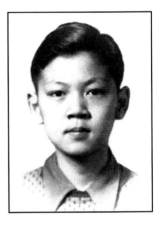

My passport photo when I left for China.

of this trip was to take Jimmy and me to China to learn the Chinese language and customs. Both my brother and I could understand a little of the Chinese language, but neither of us could speak it fluently.

Thus my journey began...

A postcard from 1940's of the Baptist Memorial Hospital in Memphis, TN where I was born.

I was born on September 23, 1935 in the Baptist Memorial Hospital in Memphis, Tennessee. Jimmy was born on October 22, 1936. We lived in Joiner, Arkansas where our Grandfather, Father (Jeu Sui Kai) and Mother owned a small grocery/drug store. When I was about two or three my father was diagnosed with tuberculosis. The nearest TB Hospital was in Little Rock, Arkansas so we moved there to admit our father for treatment.

We opened a small grocery store at the corner of 19th and Pulaski Streets. In those days in Tennessee, Arkansas and Mississippi the Chinese could only live in and operate businesses in the "colored" neighborhoods (as they were referred to back then). Our grocery store was called "Joe Jeu's Grocery Store." As you entered the front of the store, on the left there were glass counters filled with grocery items. On each side there was a counter against the wall, with high open shelf units also filled with grocery items. In the rear was a refrigerated case with a glass front where all the lunch meats, hams, chickens and other refrigerated items were kept. I remember my mother would make fried apple, peach and other fruit pies to sell. She would put them in the meat case to keep them cold. On top of the meat case were jars of sour pickles, pickled pigs feet, pickled ham hocks, link sausages and pickled eggs. Behind the meat case was the kitchen where mother made the best baked ham. She'd score the ham on top and rub some type of honey glaze all over it. When she took it out of the oven Jimmy and I couldn't wait to pinch off the top skin. It was so crunchy and smelled and tasted so good. Mother would have to make us

This is one of the few photos I have of my mother.

stop or we would have eaten all of the skin off the entire ham.

I remember the store had a small ice house in the front near the street and a chicken coop where we raised chickens at the rear of the store. Behind the kitchen was a screened-in porch. There were stairs that went down to the back yard where the chickens were kept. The back porch was about four-feet above the ground, so there was enough room for Jimmy and me to play underneath the porch. Once, we were under there playing with matches and started a fire that almost got out of hand. Thank goodness we had a water faucet near the chicken coop, we were able to put it out. Our mother never knew about that incident, thank goodness!

From underneath the porch, we could see our mother and grandfather when they would catch a chicken and "wring its neck." They would pluck all the feathers off and cook the chicken for dinner. This upset Jimmy so much he would not eat chicken for a long time. Mother would cook pork chops for him instead and Jimmy would eat them, bones and all.

On the right side of the porch was a bedroom where our mother, Jimmy and me slept. Jimmy and I slept on a small bed that was turned sideways against the foot of our mother's bed. During bed time mother would tell us about her childhood as she was growing up in China. She also told us stories that were told to her by her mother when she was little. Most of these were old Chinese fables. My favorite one was about a man with one eye in the back of his head. Many

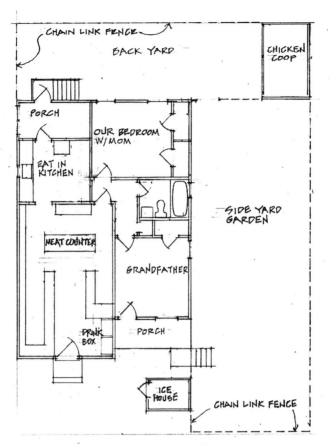

This is a rough sketch, from what I can remember, of our store and house in Little Rock, Arkansas.

nights, our Mom would tell us stories until Jimmy and I fell asleep.

Next to our bedroom, towards the front of the store was our Grandfather's bedroom. His room had a door that lead to the outside covered porch. This was where I would sit and draw from the many comic books that I had (funny books as they were called back then). I would usually draw and watch our grandfather as he tended to his garden. The garden was located in the side yard. He planted Chinese long beans, bok choy, winter melon (dong gua), green onion, Chinese cabbage (su choy), fuzzy melon (mo gua), angled loofah (suey gua), bitter melon (fu gua) and other Chinese vegetables in his garden. The garden was fenced in with a chain-link wire fence from the side yard to the front yard by the sidewalk.

I have a lot of memories from my childhood in Little Rock, playing outside and using our imaginations. Sometimes we would venture out to explore our neighborhood doing such daring acts as walking across a drainage ditch that ran through the streets. Sometimes we would climb down into the ditch and walk through it. It was really dark, but as you looked ahead, you could see light from the drain inlets. We would go from block to block and crawl out at the drain inlets. I remember one time, as we were exploring in the drainpipe, we were about in the middle of the block when a thunderstorm started. We were totally unaware of it. Then we heard a strange noise ahead of us. It was a huge surge of water coming towards us! We started running as fast as our little legs could carry us. As we came to the first street inlet we crawled out as fast as we could. This incident scared us so badly that I don't think we ever did another drainpipe exploration again.

Occasionally, we would ride the bus to the end of the line to the turn-around point. We would get off the bus and walk down the hill to the train tracks and wait for the next train to come along. Once the train slowed down to go around the curve, we would hop onto it. Many times while we waited for the train to come, we would pull up some tall weed stalks and strip them down to make pretend "spears." Then we would throw these spears at each other, like the jungle natives did in the Tarzan movies. Finally, we would see a train coming around the bend. As the train slowed down we would hop aboard an opened boxcar. We would ride it until it started to slow down, just before crossing the Arkansas River going into North Little Rock. I recall one time when we were riding the train; it did not slow down as it approached the river! Boy was I scared; my only thought at that time was, "this train probably will not stop until we get to Florida," (even though we were going north). Fortunately, the train finally did slow down in North Little Rock and we bailed out and walked across the bridge to downtown Little Rock. From there we had to get on the bus to take us back home. Boy, were we glad to be back home! I believe this ended our train adventures because we never did that again either.

We also liked to play "Tarzan" in a large tree near our house. We would climb as high as we could go up the tree, then we would hang from a branch, let go and drop, catching a lower branch. We'd continue dropping down until we finally dropped to the ground. This was one of our favorite things to do. Other times we would play "Cowboys and Indians." Once, when I was running and diving to the ground to dodge the make-believe bullets, my knee landed on a broken soda bottle and cut me really badly. I ran home and my mother had to take me to the hospital to get stitches on my cut knee. I still have that scar on my right knee to remind me of that day.

Unfortunately, that wasn't the only time I had an accident. At our store, there were two counters parallel to each other. Jimmy and I would put one hand on each counter and swing our body back and forth. One time I was swinging on the counters and my right hand slipped, I hit my head on the edge of the counter and cut my right ear. Blood was spurting everywhere. Jimmy began yelling and crying. I had to have stitches in my ear that time. But I did not swing between the counters anymore after that. I also still carry that scar on my right ear.

When we lived in Little Rock we attended Rightsell Elementary School, which was within walking distance from our house. One day I decided to skip class. Naturally the teacher called my mother to ask why I was not at school. The next day I was called into the Principal's office. As I sat in the chair facing his desk he stood up and sternly looked me in the face and said, "George, did you play hooky yesterday?" Not knowing what hooky was, I thought it was a game, so I said, "Yes Sir." Boy, I found out what hooky was when the principal finished paddling me on the behind! I was sure I would never play that game again!

Sometimes on Sundays, Jimmy and I would go to the Nabor Theater on "The Hill," as it was called then. It was about three blocks from our store. That neighborhood was up a steep hill across the streetcar line. That was also where all the "rich white folks" lived. Jimmy and I both loved to see all of the Wolfman and Frankenstein movies. After the movie, on the way home it would be getting dark, so we would always walk in the middle of the street, that way we were sure to be safe from any "monsters" that may have been lurking in the bushes next to the sidewalks. We also enjoyed seeing all of the "cowboy" movies featuring Buck Jones, Tim McCoy, Raymond Hatten, Roy Rogers, Gene Autry, "Wild Bill" Elliott and other stars. Across from the theater was a variety store that had a magazine rack at the front entrance of the store by the window. Sometimes, we would very carefully open the screen door and sit on the floor by the magazine rack to read the comic books. Unfortunately, when someone discovered us, they would make us leave.

While we were living in Little Rock, every Sunday we would go to the hospital to see our father, this was the only day we would close the store. We would travel to the hospital by bus, which would stop right in front of the hospital. After visiting with our

My Father - Jeu Sui Kai

father, our mother and grandfather would take us to a restaurant downtown that was owned by one of our cousins. We would eat a large meal and visit with our relatives until the evening.

Our father was born on August 8, 1904. He died in the hospital on January 18, 1947; he was only 42 years old. I don't recall ever seeing our father out of the hospital. My only memories of him are of us visiting him on Sundays at the hospital. Our father was buried in Little Rock, Arkansas.

After our father had passed, our grandfather

My Grandfather
Jeu Bing Fun

decided that he would return to his homeland to live out his remaining years. At that time, the Chinese people would come to America, which they referred to as "Gold Mountain" to earn a living and save money to return to China to retire. The exchange rate of Hong Kong to U.S. currency at that time was very high. Those who had children in America would establish businesses, then once their children became adults and could take over their businesses, the elders would return to China. The children would send money from the business to their parents in China to buy land and save for their retirement. By this time, our grandfather was in his 80's and he wanted to take Jimmy and me back to

Me (age 12) on the left, and Jimmy (age 11) on the right. This photo was taken in the Chong's back yard with their dog.

China with him to learn Chinese customs and language. Our mother knew that if she went back to China, she could never return to America due to the immigration laws. At that time, our cousins and friends tried to convince our mother to stay in America, but it is customary in the Chinese culture for the male to make all the family decisions. So our grandfather sold the store and started making plans to take us all to China. After selling the store we moved to Memphis, TN to stay with our cousins, Mr. and Mrs. Jeu Chong. The Chongs had a grocery store on the corner of Horn Lake Road and Peebles Avenue. This intersection was called "Grant's corner" at that time. We lived with them until our visas and passports were finalized for our trip to China, this took about a year. During our stay in Memphis, Jimmy and I started school at Levi Elementary. The school bus would pick us up in front of the Chong's grocery store. Jimmy's teacher was Mrs. Gladys Walker, who would later become a very crucial part of our lives, yet at the time we did not know it.

At Levi we met some of our cousins attending school there. They were living with another cousin, Mr. K.C. Fong, who lived close to the Chong's grocery store, so they could go to school in Memphis. They were from Lake Cormorant, Mississippi where they could not attend the "white schools" due to the Mississippi laws. The Chinese people could only go to the "colored schools" as they were called back then. Our cousins from Lake Cormorant, Mississippi were Jimmy, George, Roosevelt, B.B., Sue and Tom Tong. They also had another brother Willie, who was living in China. Due to immigration laws, Willie could not come to America because he was born in China. They had to leave him behind in the care of other relatives.

Interestingly, the Tongs and the Chongs were really from the Jeu family, but they used their father's first name as their last name. The immigration laws at that time were very difficult for the Chinese who came to America. If any discrepancies appeared in their papers or passports they could possibly be denied entry into America. It was customary in China, to always say or write your surname first followed by your first name. At the immigration office, the officers interrupted the Chinese people's names in the American tradition with their first name first and then their surname. So when their dads, Jeu Tong and Jeu Chong came to America their names were not transposed at the immigration office, which made Tong and Chong their surnames in America. I have many relatives living in America whose names are turned around because they were afraid to say anything, for fear of being denied entry into America.

I enjoyed the weekends when our grandfather would take Jimmy and me to downtown Memphis to the Chinese Club, the "Lung Kong Tin Yee Association" on Vance Avenue. The Association was on the north side of Vance Avenue near Third Street. It was in a two-story building with two businesses on the ground floor. Between the two businesses was a stairway that led up to the entry to the Association on the second floor. There was also a store on the corner of Third Street that the youngsters would go to and buy candy and ice cream.

The Chinese Association was established by the local Chinese community and people such as my grandfather, Charlie Wah and Mr. Lock of Hughes, Arkansas. It was originally set up to help Chinese immigrants find jobs and start their own businesses such as restaurants and grocery stores. There were bedrooms at the clubhouse where immigrants could use until they could get out on their own. Money was also made available to them through loans from the member's donations to the Association. As you climbed the steep staircase to enter the Association, there were rooms on each side of the stairs and a large room facing Vance Avenue. Sometimes as you looked down from the second floor onto Vance Avenue, you would see "street walkers" (prostitutes) across the street. Towards the rear on the left, was a large room that had bunk beds where people could rest or spend the night. On the right side was the "Mahjong Room," where the adults would play Mahjong. There were about eight to ten tables in that room. Each table would seat four people. Some would play for fun, while others were serious players who gambled with high stakes. Thousands of dollars would be at risk. I once heard a player had won enough to buy a car! Gambling was illegal at that time, but outsiders did not know about the "Mahjong Room."

Mahjong game set. A game using ivory tiles with three suits, winds, dragons and flowers that are used to make sets or runs of three. (Similar to Rummy)

Many Chinese banquets would be held there for New Years, birthdays, baby parties and wedding banquets as well as other special events. The various banquets at the Chinese Club will forever be some of my fondest memories of the Chinese Community in Memphis. Everyone would volunteer to help. Days before an event, members would volunteer to clean the banquet room and prepare the food to be cooked. There were many preparations to be done, such as cutting the meats, washing and chopping the vegetables, marinating the pork, duck and chicken and soaking the dried black mushrooms and other dried herbs and items that had to be prepared ahead of time before cooking. The young boys would roll out four-foot round plywood tabletops and set them on top of square folding tables, then ten to twelve metal folding chairs would be placed at each table. Plastic table cloths would be placed on the tables, then the young girls would set the tables with silverware, bowls, plates, chop sticks cups and napkins. Bottles of soft drinks would be put in the Coca-Cola coolers and iced down. After everything was done some of the adults would remain and play Mahjong until the wee hours of the morning. Some of these men would be the cooks, as they would stay and start preparing the dishes that had to cook for hours ahead of time for the banquets.

As people arrived to the banquets, they would find a table for their family, on some occasions tables would be assigned to each family. A stage about three-feet high, with steps on each end, was at the rear of the dining room. This is where the President and Officers of the Association or Banquet Host would welcome everyone. Honored guests would be introduced; companies and individuals who donated food, drinks and other supplies would also be acknowledged and thanked. All of the speeches would be spoken in Chinese (Cantonese) and then translated into English.

On the left side of the dining room was the kitchen. The kitchen had a walk-in cooler at one end. Against one wall were four large woks and large sinks. Along the other wall was a long counter top with cabinets below for storing dishes, bowls, silverware, chopsticks and other kitchen items. Above the counter top was a large pass through window opening into the dining room. The pass through had a shelf that was used to set the dishes on, as they were prepared and ready to serve. The cooks would place the finished dishes on the shelf and the young men on the other side would pick them up and take them to the tables.

It was customary for the men to do the cooking, each had their specialty dish that they would take charge of preparing. Soup would be the first dish to be served. It was usually Bird's Nest Soup, one of my favorite soups, also a Chinese delicacy. Then other dishes would be served, such as mixed vegetables with shrimp or other meats, chicken, roasted duck, barbecue pork (char su), black mushrooms, a thin vermicelli-like mung bean noodle dish called saifun, ketchup shrimp, abalone, squid and other delicious dishes. There were always an uneven number of courses served, either seven or nine. All dishes were served in large bowls or plates and were set on the table to be shared family style. You would go to the drink coolers for your drinks. Sometimes there would be so many guests, that there would have to be a second shift to accommodate the large number of guests. Families from Mississippi and Arkansas would usually be invited also. All of the out-of-town guest would be served on the first shift so they could start their journey home before it got too late. After dinner, everyone would be given take-out containers for their leftovers. The young teenagers would clear the tables after the first shift and set up for the second shift. Once everyone had eaten, the young people would take down the tables and fold up the chairs and return everything to the storage area. The floor would then be mopped and cleaned. Once the cleanup was done, some adults would stay late and play Mahjong.

These events would normally last all day so people could stay and visit their cousins and friends from Tennessee, Mississippi and Arkansas. It was a great way to stay in touch with extended family members and friends.

When we went to the clubhouse, we would ride the trolley to Main Street and get off in front of the Malco Theater. We would walk down Beale Street to 2nd Street then to Vance. That is where the clubhouse was. Sometimes our grandfather would take us to the Chop Suey Café on Beale Street, which was owned by our cousins Mr. and Mrs. Jeu Sing. We would stay with them while our grandfather would go to the clubhouse to play Mahjong and visit with other Chinese men. Mrs. Jeu Sing would make us a bowl of noodle soup or some other delicious Chinese dish. I remember eating chow mein noodles that she stored in a large barrel in the kitchen. The Chop Suey Café catered mostly to the blacks, as most of the businesses' did on Beale Street in those days. Mr. Jeu Sing had some tables in the kitchen that he used for the few white people that came in the back door to order lunch or dinner.

I remember when Jimmy and I went downtown, as we got onto the trolley; I wasn't sure where we should sit. I found us a seat between the white people who sat in the front, and the colored people who sat in the back. Since we were Chinese, I wasn't sure where we were supposed to sit so we always sat in the row in the middle.

The S.S. President Wilson II Cruise Liner

Once our papers were finally cleared, we left Memphis on our way to China. We sailed from San Francisco on board the S.S. President Wilson II American President Lines. The voyage across the Pacific Ocean seemed to go by quickly, although it actually took three weeks.

There are only a few things I can remember about the voyage. One was playing the slot machines. Jimmy must have hit a jackpot because dimes kept falling into the hopper. Another memory I have was the swimming pool. I had put a life ring around my waist because I could not swim so I could jump off the diving board. But as I jumped up and down on the diving board, the ring slid off my waist and down to my knees just before I entered the water. I came up, bottom first and I thought I was going to drown!

As we approached Hawaii, young men and boys were in the ocean swimming out to the boat to greet us. Passengers were throwing coins into the ocean and the men would dive down and retrieve them. We stopped in Hawaii and were allowed to go ashore to sightsee and purchase souvenirs. Jimmy and I bought Hawaiian shirts that were very colorful and flowery. After leaving Hawaii we stopped in Manila, in the Philippines. We were not allowed to go ashore there because of the destruction from World War II. But from the ship we could see all of the bombed buildings, charred trees and huge holes in the ground from the bombs. After an overnight stay in the harbor, we continued on our voyage to China.

We finally arrived in Hong Kong. In the harbor there were many boats of all sizes. Some were houseboats that people lived on. We could see them on their boats cooking their meals. And I remember seeing their clothes hanging on lines to dry. Some of the boats were floating restaurants, some were small and some were very large and ornate with huge flags. Our uncle, Jeu Sui Yee met us as we came ashore and took us to a hotel. After we checked in and got settled into our room, our uncle took us to a restaurant. This was my first dim sum meal. Dim sum is served during tea time. The foods are usually small bite-sized portions of steamed or fried dumplings with pork, shrimp and vegetables wrapped in a rice flour skin or noodle. Some that I remember were, lo mai gai - a sticky rice with meat wrapped in lotus leaves, cheung fun - meats rolled in rice noodles, don tot - flaky, egg custard tarts and chicken's feet that were stir fried, marinated and steamed. During dinner, our uncle told our mother to keep us near her and to hold our hands while we were sightseeing, as there were people who would try to kidnap us and hold us for ransom. Our mother held on to us tightly everywhere we went after that.

Hong Kong was so different from Memphis. There were so many people of so many different races – I remember seeing Chinese, Indians from India with their turbans on their heads, English, Portuguese and African people. People were walking in the streets and on the sidewalks. There were two-tiered buses, cars and rickshaws everywhere. As we walked along the street we could see roasted ducks and geese hanging in the windows of stores. There were Chinese medicine shops and we could smell the aroma of foods being cooked by street vendors. Noodle soups, fried rice dishes and stir fried meat and vegetables dishes. You could order whatever you wanted and eat it right there from a bowl with a pair of chopsticks. Hong Kong was truly a memorable experience for me.

We finally left Hong Kong and boarded a large ferry for Macao, a Portuguese port on mainland China; from there we boarded a small boat to Canton. This boat was operated by men on each side who used long bamboo poles to propel the boat down the river.

Upon our arrival in Canton, we hired men with rickshaws to take us to Jiangmen. This is the name of the town after the Communist took over and the Mandarin language became the main dialect of China. I don't remember the Cantonese name for this town; I think this was the closest town to our village at that time. I remember seeing many people begging in the streets. There were some that were maimed and homeless. Our uncle told us to avoid them. The rickshaws that we rode in were pulled by one man on foot, who held two long poles extending from the front of the rickshaw. There were about eight rickshaws in all, three for the family and the others for our belongings; suit cases, trunks, gifts for our Aunt and cousins and also a large amount of food items purchased in Jiangmen for the customary banquet planned for our arrival.

The rice fields outside our village.

People in the village working with the rice.

The trip to the village was about four-and-a-half to five hours along a winding dirt road about six feet wide with an occasional cut across the path for drainage from the rice fields on both sides. We could see mountains and small villages in the distance. We saw people working in some of the rice fields along the way. All of the workers were wearing similar clothing; dark, long sleeved shirts, baggy pants and wide brimmed straw hats. Later, I found out that all the pants came in one size. You would double them up in the front, left to right, then roll them down around your belt or a string. What a sight Jimmy and I must have been, wearing our Levi jeans and brightly colored Hawaiian shirts!

Approaching the front of our village there was a ten to twelve-foot high wall the width of the village.

The entrance to our Village.

The photo on the left is the walk way between the houses.
The photo on the right is the back of the house.

The scrolls of bright red paper are hung over the door and
on each side to bring blessings to the family who lives there.

There were two massive gates. Above the doors there was some large Chinese calligraphy that said the name of our village "Long Tin Lay," with carved dragons and other ornate decorations. On the right side of the village was a huge forest of bamboo. The bamboo was so thick you could not see through it. The bamboo went along the full length of the village. On the left side was a pond about 50-feet wide that went the length of the village. This was full of fish that the villagers used for food. As you entered the main street you could see the rear entrance in the distance. The main Street was about 15-20 feet wide. On each side were rows of single-story, row-houses (similar to American town houses.) All the roofs were red clay tile. The front entry of each house would face the rear exit of the next house. The Chinese custom required all front entries to the houses to face the east with the rising sun. It is believed to enhance the occupant's good fortune and good health.

As our uncle led us down the main street, we turned right at the second row of houses from the back of the village. Our house was the third house from the main street. As we approached the front of the house, there were a pair of large wooden doors with 12-inch wide red paper scrolls with black Chinese writing on them hanging on each side. The writing was to protect the inhabitants of the house from evil spirits, wishing them good fortune, good health and longevity. These scrolls were on the front entry of all of the houses and

Looking through the house from the front doorway.

The atrium area.

were replaced periodically as they began to fade. As we entered the house, straight ahead you could see the back door. On our right was a living unit which consisted of a living room and bed room, on the left was the dining area which was part of the entry way. Continuing on, you came to an open atrium in the center of the house. On the right side of the atrium was the large living unit, which contained the customary Chinese family altar with red paper scrolls, photos of ancestors and incense holders. This unit also had a living

The family alter inside the house.

room and a large bedroom. On the left of the atrium was a small kitchen. In this room there were two large woks where all the food was prepared. Beneath them were two openings, where a fire was built using rice straw that was stored on the opposite end of the kitchen. Past the atrium was a storage area and the back exit of the house.

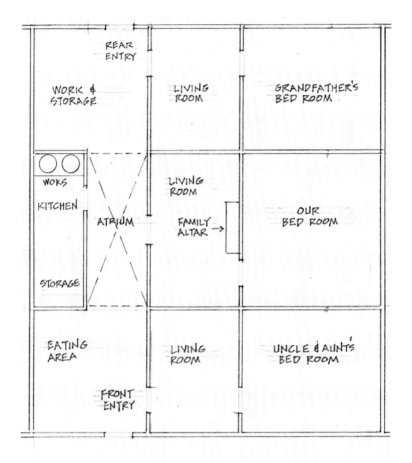

FLOOR PLAN OF HOUSE IN CHINA
(AS I REMEMBER IT - ROOM SIZES MAY VARY)

On the right was another living unit with a living room and a bedroom.

According to Chinese customs the first-born son inhabits the large middle living unit of the house. Since my father was the first-born son and he had passed, I inherited the unit as my father's first-born son. My uncle had been living there while we were in America, but he and his family had to move out upon our arrival. I never knew how my uncle, aunt and all of their children were able to sleep in their small unit. I don't recall ever going in there. Our grandfather moved into the small rear unit.

Outside of the rear entry, to the left, was a large single story building. This was where all of the banquets were held for weddings, birthdays, baby parties, new years and other events. It was customary for the entire village to participate in these functions. The men would do all the cooking. The women would help with chopping the food to be cooked and everyone would help set up tables and chairs and clean up afterwards. On the right side, across from the Banquet hall was another large one-story building for the men to play Mahjong, Chinese Chess and card games. We never went into this building, as children were not allowed to enter it. Later I found out they also smoked opium in there. Outside the rear entry wall was a statue of Buddha, about six feet tall. In the distance you could see another village about a mile away at the foot of the mountain and between the villages there were rice fields.

As my brother and I settled into our new home, in a new country, we would soon start school and begin the task of learning the language and customs of our parents. Little did we know at that time, what an amazing journey that was going to be.

When I was in China, this was near the back gate of the village where a six-foot tall statue of Buddha was. It has deteriorated over the years since I was there. Only the wall around it is still in tact.

My Journey

Part 2
The Village of "Long Tin Lay"

It had been quite an adjustment period for Jimmy and me since we arrived in China from America. Living in the village was like taking a step "back in time." Life there was very hard for most of the villagers. There were no jobs except in nearby towns, which were miles away. Everyone who lived in the village was a farmer. Most villagers did not have money so they would swap their harvested crops for food and other staples that they needed.

There was no electricity, no running water and no gas in our village. We were not used to living without electricity or running water like we had in Memphis. The only light we had was from oil lamps. There weren't any light switches or electrical outlets. No radios, TVs or other electrical items. All of the rooms were dark and musty due to the lack of light and windows. The houses did not have windows in any of the rooms because the sides of the house were common walls between the houses next to it. You only had the front and rear doors to open during the day to get sunlight into the house. The only other light in the rooms was from the natural light that came in from the open atrium in the center of the house.

There was no running water in the houses so all of our water was drawn from a common well in the village and brought to our house by the women every day for cooking and cleaning. There were no inside bathrooms. You would use a clay pot with a lid on it in your living unit. These pots were emptied every morning in a common area at the rear of the village. Boy, was I glad to be a male because emptying the pots was one of the duties of the females of the family, along with cooking and washing all the clothes. Upon awakening in the morning, you would wash yourself in your living unit, using a small pan of water and bar of soap. I remember our aunt would always tell us to not leave the soap in the water when we washed ourselves, because soap was very expensive. It took some getting used to taking a bath from a bucket of water instead of having a bathtub to sit in.

There was a common toilet near the banquet building in the rear of the village, which made it convenient during banquets. It was built over the stream, so that what ever went in the toilet fell into the water.

This is the well that our water was drawn from.

Most times the clothes were taken to a near by stream to be washed. This stream was also where we would catch fish. We would get large rocks and lay them across the stream and then we would dig up the dirt and mud from the bottom and pack the mud between the rocks to build a dam. Others would do the same to create a dam up stream. Once both dams were constructed, we would open a small section of the lower dam to release the water. When the water had finally drained out, we would quickly pick up all the fish that were trapped before the upper dam overflowed. Sometimes we would even catch a few shrimp or eels.

All of our beds were made of wood, maybe teakwood, with a very ornate carved headboard. Above the headboard was a canopy to hold the insect netting that was secured around the perimeter of the canopy. The base around the bed was completely enclosed with ornately carved wood panels to keep any pests from getting underneath the bed. The beds were usually pushed into a corner of the room to provide more space for other furniture. The beds had a thin mattress made from cloth and stuffed with some type of soft material. I remember the bedroom was always dark. When you went to bed you would get inside the netting and tuck it underneath the mattress to keep insects from entering. After awakening in the morning, you would bundle the bottom of the netting tightly together and tie it into a loose knot, thus preventing mosquitoes and other insects from getting inside the netting during the day. At that time

Inside the bed with the netting hanging down.

the Chinese also used wood blocks that were curved at the top for pillows. It was about the size of a large loaf of bread. I sure was glad we brought our own fluffy soft pillows from America!

Since there was no electricity, there were no refrigerators available, most of our food items were dried or preserved if they were not fresh from our garden. Our aunt always tried to cook only enough for one meal so there would be no left overs except for rice. The left over rice was not a problem because she could use it to make fried rice for the next meal or rice soup called jook, which is rice porridge.

There were no telephones or electricity for radios in our village. All news, of any importance would come to us by word-of-mouth from people who would go to the city of Jiangmen for shopping. They would bring back newspapers and share any news that was told to them by people living in the city. Mail was not delivered to the rural villages where we lived either. Any mail received from over-seas relatives had to be picked up in Jiangmen weekly or monthly during our shopping trips. The nearest telephones were in the cities of Jiangmen or Canton. There were also no motorized vehicles in our village. We had to walk everywhere we went. We even walked to the market when we went shopping and the nearest market was about one mile away.

My uncle was the Mayor of the village because he was one of the few elders living there who had a college education. While we were living in America, our father and grandfather had sent much of their money to China for my uncle to put into the British bank in Hong Kong to help support our relatives and to save for our grandfather's return to China. One never deposited money from America into Chinese banks because of the instability of the Chinese currency at that time. When you did exchange U.S. currency into Chinese currency, you only exchanged exactly what you needed. It was possible for the currency to be declared void and worthless the very next day without warning so any money you had left would be useless. My uncle used the money my grandfather and father had sent to China, to go to college and obtain a degree. He also sent his oldest son, Jeu Mun Jip to college and who became the teacher in the village school. He was the only teacher in our village so he taught all of the children, from first through fifth grades.

In China you could only go to school if your family could afford to pay for it. Families would pay our uncle with bushels of rice for their children's tuition for school. In turn, our uncle would swap the rice for meat and vegetables or pay others to work in our rice fields. Adjusting to the school in our village was really difficult for both Jimmy and me. It was bad enough that we did not know the language and could barely understand it, but the school was so different from what we had known at Levi. The school was located outside the main entrance of the village. It was a small one-room building with small garden plots on one side where the students were taught to plant gardens and grow vegetables such as bok choy, long beans, bitter melon, winter melon, green onion and other Chinese vegetables. Every morning we would do exercises before class.

The language was so difficult to learn because there is no alphabet in the Chinese language. They

The school house as it looks today.
When we were there, it was only the building on the right.

use characters more like hieroglyphics. You had to memorize every character. There are literally thousands of characters in the Chinese language. Also in Chinese schools students were required to study "out loud." Boy, that really took some getting used to! Imagine trying to concentrate while everyone in the class is reading and studying out loud!

Even though we were in the sixth grade in school when we left America, Jimmy and I had to start back in the first grade in China because we did not know the language. Consequently, we both failed our first year. Slowly, but finally, we learned to converse in Chinese with the help of our cousins and classmates. During this period we would receive letters and gifts from Mrs. Gladys Walker, Jimmy's teacher from Levi Elementary School and some of his classmates. My most prized possessions I had at that time were a Boy Scout Manual, a Bible Mrs. Walker sent to us, and some books by O. Henry, Jack London and Mark Twain. I really enjoyed reading those books we received from America!

Mrs. Walker started a pen pal club to keep in touch with Jimmy while we were in China. The students would send us Christmas cards, baseball gloves, balls and other things from America that we couldn't get in China. We would write letters back to the students to let them know how we were doing and tell them about our life in China.

Jimmy and I were slowly becoming accustomed to our new life here in the little village of Long Tin Lay. We finally started venturing outside the village walls, but were sternly warned by everyone to be inside the village before dark. We were told of bandits who roamed the countryside at night looking for someone that they could capture and hold for ransom, especially those who came from America. Some of the villagers told stories about a large serpent that roams the rice fields at night and would catch anyone that was out at night and kill and eat them. Believe me, we made certain that we were always inside the walls of the village before night fell!

Sometimes you could hear gunfire from a nearby village. I remember one time some men were on the roof of the banquet hall repairing the roof tiles when all of the sudden they heard bullets bouncing all around them. Someone was shooting from the mountains. They all immediately jumped to the ground. Thank goodness no one was hurt.

Another time Jimmy and I were outside the rear entry of our village playing near the statue of Buddha. Jimmy decided he would climb on the statue. Boy was that a mistake, villagers were running towards us and yelling at us. I couldn't understand a word they were saying but I knew it wasn't good. You see, Buddha is a very sacred symbol to the Chinese people and you are absolutely NOT to climb on him! We never did that again. In fact we hardly ever went near that statue again.

Working in the rice fields was another experience I will always remember. Planting stalks of rice seedlings in soft muddy fields, with water above your feet. "What is that stinging sensation on my foot?" As

I raised my foot to examine it, there was a worm-like thing stuck to my foot. I started yelling to my cousin nearby. He ran over to me and quickly took me to the path where he pulled the creature off my foot and smashed it with a rock. Blood spurted everywhere. It was a leech, a blood-sucking worm! Boy, was I apprehensive about getting back into the water after that. During harvest time we would cut down the rice stalks and tie them up into bundles about the width of a barrel and four-feet tall. Then we would take a long pole with pointed ends and shove each end into each of the bundles. You would get between the bundles, underneath the pole and lift them up onto your shoulders so you could carry the rice bundles to your house in the village, which as about 100 yards away. Believe me, it seemed like five miles to me!

This was something I never could get used to. My shoulders would ache for days. When you walk with these rice bundles on the pole you would tend to sway from side to side and the bundles would bounce up and down which made it very difficult to walk. My cousin told me not to bounce so much. Easy for him to say. "You

Carrying pole similar to the ones we used.

have to walk with a steady gait so the bundles won't bounce up and down. That is why your shoulders are hurting," he would tell me. And just think, this was how the girls got water from the well in the village every morning after emptying the toilet pots. They would carry one bucket of water on each end of the pole, with each bucket holding about five gallons of water!

Once we carried the rice back to our house, we would untie the bundles and lay them out to dry. When the rice stalks were dry, we would beat them over a screen type structure to knock the rice kernels off into a pan below the screen. The rice was then put into a round stone structure with grooves in it with another similar stone lowered on top of it. The top stone had a handle on it that you would push as you walked around the structure. This was how the husks were separated from the rice kernels. Then all of the rice and husks were picked up and put into a

Stone like the one we used to remove husks from the rice kernels.

large rattan bowl about three-feet across. There was fan suspended from the ceiling that was made from a large rectangular rattan piece, about six-feet wide by two-feet with a rope on each end. One person with the rattan bowl would toss the rice and husks into the air, another person would pull the ropes to fan the rice. The fan would blow the husks away and the rice would fall back down into the bowl. The rice was then put into large clay containers with tops and stored in the kitchen area until needed.

Jimmy and I taught our cousins and other boys in the village how to play baseball. There was an open yard behind the banquet hall with a basketball goal. This was where the children would play their games. They taught us how to play a Chinese stick game similar to baseball, Mahjong, Chinese chess and other games. There weren't many days that we had the luxury of "play time" like we had back in Memphis where we would play baseball in the cotton fields behind our cousin's grocery store. One of the boys we met in the village in China was a cousin of ours. His English name was Willie Tong. I don't recall his Chinese name. He was the brother of Jimmy, George and Roosevelt Tong who we had attend Levi School with in Memphis. He was the brother who had been born in China when his parents had come to visit and could not go to America with them when they went back due to the immigration laws at that time. We became good friends with Willie while we were in China. Fortunately, later he was allowed to go to America to live with his family.

One of my fondest memories from America was going with my cousin George Tong from Lake Cormorant, Mississippi to the movies at the Malco Theater. We would catch the trolley at the turn around loop in south Memphis and ride to downtown Memphis. We would get off at Main Street and Beale and walk to Krystal hamburger restaurant at Second or Third street. George would order two-dozen hamburgers and french fries. We would sneak these into the Malco Theater and sit in the balcony, where we would feast on the burgers during the movie. George Tong was built like a football lineman and he would eat at least 18 of the Krystals while I would try to finish off the remaining six. Whew! Sometime we would go to a second movie at another movie theater: The Princess, The Warner, Lowe's Palace or Lowe's State. I really missed going to the movies and riding the trolley downtown to see Mr. and Mrs. Jeu Sing at the Chop Suey Café and I really missed eating those chow mein noodles Mrs. Jeu Sing cooked for us.

How could life here be so different from the life that we had in America? I often wondered why my grandfather and mother wanted to come back to China. I was too young to know the real reason. At least we had the letters from Mrs. Walker and Jimmy's classmates to keep us tied to our former life in America.

As time went by we got more accustomed to the slow pace of life in rural China. We would go to the market about once a month to get the necessities that we needed. Usually our uncle would take my brother

Jimmy, some of his sons and me with him. Our aunt would stay at home with the girls and one of the older sons. They had three sons, Mun Jip, Mun Oui and Mun Gin and four daughters Boi Fay, Boi Fong, Boi Hing and Boi Git.

My Uncle's family. They had three sons and four daughters. We are standing on the back row (from left to right) one of my Uncle's daughters, my brother Jimmy, Mun Jip - my Uncle's oldest son the school teacher, me and then two other sons.

When we went to the market shopping, the first place we would go to was a Tea House to "yum cha" (drink tea) and eat dim sum. Sometimes we would also get jook (rice porridge soup) like my aunt made. The dim sum servings consist of three or four small pieces of each dish, which is shared by everyone at the table. I remember eating shu mai (steamed pork dumplings), har gow (shrimp dumplings), char siu bao (steamed pork buns), pai gwat (steamed riblets in black bean sauce), wu gok (deep fried taro balls), lo mai gai (sticky rice and veggies wrapped in lotus leaves), don tot (egg custard tarts) and many more items. There would be pushcarts filled with small round bamboo steamer containers that were stacked on top of each other. Each small steamer contained different dishes. The carts would be pushed around the room from table to table and you would pick what you wanted to order from the cart when it was at your table. I enjoyed this so much! Then we would shop for items such as soy sauce, oyster sauce, hoisin sauce, sesame oil, dried oysters, dried shrimp and canned items for cooking. Our uncle always bought "Hi-Ho" crackers from America; these must have been one of his favorite snacks. He also bought other things that our aunt had requested. Sometimes he would

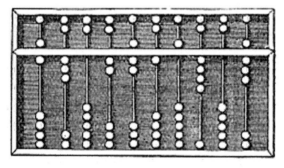

Abacus similar to the one the merchants used for calculating the total of our purchases. We learned how to count on these in school.

stop at the Chinese medicine shops where you could see shelves of dried roots, leaves, insects, snakes and other strange things. All of the merchants in the stores would total up our purchases on an abacus, a calculating instrument using rows of beads that slide up or down on rods to add and subtract. They could do this as fast as people using an adding machine. The shopping trip would usually take us all day.

The first year in China was a very exciting time for us. We were experiencing so many new things and learning so much about our heritage and the Chinese culture. I finally learned how to carry the rice straw on a pole on my shoulder, but I still didn't like it. I also began to get used to pulling the leeches off my feet during planting season. And in our small garden plots at school I was learning how to grow many different Chinese vegetables.

We did not know then, how the Communist soldiers that were coming in from the North, would soon affect our lives. Our journey would soon be drastically changed.

A letter Jimmy and I wrote to Mrs. Walker while in China. June 9, 1949. She had kept it all these years.

Long Tin Lee
Kuting Sun Wai
June 9, 1949

Dear Mrs. Walker,

We got your letter and enjoy reading it. Our school isn't out yet. We are not getting along fine in China The Russians have fought and won Shanghai not long ago next is going to be Canton. Everybody is scared because they heard the ~~soldiers~~ people talking about the ~~Russian~~ Russians catching all the old people and pushing them in Rivers and Lakes and seperate one family one in one place and the others in another place.

I'm sorry to tell you our uncle doesn't like us much since we came back to China. He has been trying to get our money. When our Mother and Grandfather died he was very happy Right now he is trying to get all of our good things. When our mother died we were building a house. and now our Uncle is trying to get it. He won't let us send much letters now. He said it waste too much money. That is why we ask you for the notebooks, and things.

Jimmy said tell Ronnie D. and Ronnie E. to write to him some time.

We don't know when we will come back to America. Tell George Tom that we thank him a lot for buying the notebooks and paper and we also thank you very much, Mrs. Walker. Tell every one to write to us every once in a while.

We wish every minute that we were in America. We come back to China to have bad luck. We know how to play basketball very good now. Next year we will live in our new house.

Mrs. Walker, Next time if you send anything to us write to us and tell us about it. We love you very much, Mrs. Walker. We wish we were over there with you every minute.

With Much Love,
George and Jimmy

P.S. You don't have to worry about us Mrs. Walker, all of our neighbors know how we all is. All of our neighbor is good (our friend) we will come to say too. We like them very much. (back to America in the 5 years)

My Journey

Part 3
Under Communist Rule

There was a lot of apprehension in the country, especially in the rural areas due to the difficulties of receiving information. There were many rumors going around about the Communist government and all of the changes they were making in the cities and villages. Since there was no way for us to get the news in the village from radios we would rely on getting information from people as they passed by the village on their way south to Hong Kong or Macao.

Our lives continued as we were living in the village and we were slowly becoming accustomed to the daily rituals of our new life in China. After some months, our grandfather told us that he was going to get married again. He said that he needed someone to take care of him in his old age. It was customary in China for older widowers to marry women to care for them in their declining years. Our grandfather also said that we would be moving to the city of Jiangmen, our mother was planning to build Jimmy and me each a two-story building there. Our mom had envisioned plans for us to live on the second floor and have a business on the ground floor or rent it to someone. So we moved into an apartment building near the site of our future home. About a

This is the only photo we have of the building that my mother had built for us in Jiangmen. We never saw it or got to live there. I've been told that it is no longer there. We are still trying to find out if I still own the property or the buildings that were built to replace this one.

month or so after we moved, our mother got sick with pneumonia and eventually was taken to the hospital. The doctor told us she was very sick, so our uncle came to stay with us. One day the doctor summoned us to come to the hospital to our mom's room because she wanted to talk to us. She told me that if we ever went back to America to always visit our Father's graveside in Little Rock. And if something happened to her, I was to take care of Jimmy. I promised her that I would, but I wondered as I made this vow to her if we would ever see America again. Within days our mother passed away. I have often wondered if this would have happened if we had not come to China. I sincerely believed that she could have recovered from the pneumonia if we were still in America with more modern medicines and living conditions. How could this be happening to us? Our father had died in Little Rock and now here in China our mother has died. I was only 14 years old and Jimmy was 13. We only had our grandfather left, who was now in his 80s. Who would take care of us? What would happen to us now? We had a small ceremony for my mother attended by our uncle, Jimmy and me. We buried my mother in Jiangmen. Then our uncle moved us back to the village, back into our grandfather's house.

We started going to the school in the village where our cousin taught. I remember in school, learning and practicing to write Chinese characters. We had a bound book of rice paper sleeves, which were transparent. You would insert a sheet of printed Chinese characters into a rice paper sleeve and copy the character on the transparent sleeve. We would use a calligraphy brush with a bamboo holder and black ink that was ground from an ink block for these practices.

A sample page from my school practice book.

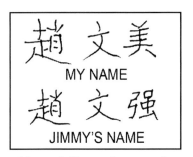

MY NAME

JIMMY'S NAME

My and Jimmy's name in Chinese characters.

I really enjoyed these exercises and eventually I learned the proper way to write using the Chinese Calligraphy.

One day we were told that the Nationalist Chinese army troops would be marching close to our village as they retreated to the south. We never saw any troops, although you could hear faint sounds of shooting in the distance. As the days went by, Communist troops would stop by our village and meet with our uncle and other elders to tell them what to expect from the new government. We were ordered to clean up the village, sweep the main street and all of the pathways. We were also told that the Communist government would be appointing people who would be responsible for making sure that all government orders were carried out in the villages. All children must now attend school and would be required to read from the "Little Red Book," which were statements from speeches and writings by Mao Zedong, the leader of the Communist Party. We would be expected to memorize quotes that were read to us. Occasionally we would have parades during the school year. Because I was the tallest student in school, I was selected to carry the Communist Flag at the front of every parade. The only musical instruments that I can recall during these parades were drums. We would sing and quote out loud the sayings from Mao Zedong's Little Red Book.

All of the villagers would be summoned periodically to the market place in Gui Jing to listen to speeches from the communist officers in charge of our area. Sometimes people would bring charges against the large landowners who had mistreated them in the past. If the landowner was found guilty of the wrong he had been accused of by a panel of villagers that was selected by the officer in charge, the landowner would be sent to prison or worst yet, he would be executed by a firing squad. There was so much propaganda and uncertainty during that time, many people were afraid to voice their opinions to anyone. You could not complain about how things were because "those in charge" had secretly picked people in all of the villages to be their contact sources and spies. The spies would tell the men in charge the names of the people who were still sympathizers of Chiang Kai-sheik, the leader of the Nationalist Government. The spies would tell the men in charge who the large landowners were and if they had mistreated any of the poorer residents. They would also inform the men in charge of which villagers had relatives that were still members of the Nationalist party. It was true that some of the affluent residents in some of the villages had taken advantage of the poor for years. Sometimes we would hear about some of these landlords being executed in the market place in front of all the villagers who were brought there to be witnesses and to be intimidated by these acts.

About a year after my mother had died, my grandfather also died. He was buried in the village cemetery. I remember that his funeral ceremony was very elaborate. A paper house, paper money and paper furniture were burned so he would have them in his after life. Real food was prepared and placed at his grave along with burning incense sticks. All of which was customary in the Chinese culture. After my grandfather had passed, my new grandmother moved back to her village. I don't know if this was a mutual agreement between our uncle and her, or why she left. I am sorry that I had not gotten to know her better during the short time she was there. I recall, she took really good care of our grandfather and they both seemed to be so happy together.

I began to sense a change in my uncle's attitude towards Jimmy and me. His father had brought his sister-in-law and two boys back from America to a changing country where the future was uncertain. There would no longer be money coming to him from America. We began to see his resentment towards us. In the Chinese culture, since I was the first-born son of my father, who was my grandfather's first-born son, I should now be the head of the family, but I was only 15. My uncle had the responsibility of his own family and now two more children. What was he going to do with us?

This is when fate stepped in – I firmly believe this. There were rumors coming from people that returned from shopping in Jiangmen, that the Communist Party was going to "liquidate" all American born

Chinese people. By liquidate, they meant "put to death." Based on these rumors, true or not, my uncle decided that he needed to get us out of China as quickly as possible. Since my uncle was the Mayor of our village, he had access to people who could help us. He immediately went to Hong Kong and was able to secure passage for us on the next to the last ship that would be allowed to leave China headed to San Francisco. He said had also made arrangements with a cousin to meet us in San Francisco upon our arrival in America. When my uncle returned to the village he gave us instructions on what we needed to do. He told us that we could not pack too much or take things that one would normally take on a long voyage, like when we arrived in China. We would have to leave everything behind that we had brought with us. We could only pack a few things so that it would appear that we were just going on a shopping trip to Canton. Then my uncle gave us both $5 in U.S. currency to put into our shoe. I wondered why this sum of money? Was that all the U.S. currency that he had at the time? How long was that supposed to last us? My uncle secretly secured us passage on a small boat from Macao to Hong Kong. As we were crossing the Hong Kong harbor a Communist patrol boat stopped us. The Communist troops boarded the boat and ordered the ship's captain to line up all the passengers into two rows to be interrogated and searched. What would happen to us if they found the U.S. money in our shoes? The soldiers began searching the passengers. We were standing in the back row. Right before the soldiers got to us, the officer in charge recognized my uncle. They had gone to college together. They talked a while and then the officer told the other soldiers to let us pass. How can I explain my feelings about this incredible experience? A blessing? I often wondered what would have happened to us if that officer had not known our uncle.

Due to the delay caused by the search, when we arrived at the harbor in Hong Kong, we had missed our ship. Some how, our uncle managed to get us on board the next voyage which was the "last ship" being allowed to leave Hong Kong, the S.S. President Cleveland. I was so relieved as we walked up the gangplank. Jimmy did not want to leave. He said, "What are we going to do? We are all alone, we should stay in China with our uncle." I told him that we needed to go back to America. We would have a greater chance to better ourselves. There was nothing back in the village for us now. Our mother and grandfather were gone and we had to leave. I literally had to drag him on board the ship with me.

Now my brother and I began our journey back to America, this time alone...

The last ship allowed to leave China, The S.S. President Cleveland. Jimmy and I boarded with one suitcase and $5 each, not knowing what lay ahead for us in America.

My Journey

Part 4
Back Home to Memphis, Tennessee

The voyage back to America on board the S. S. President Cleveland was a very emotional time for me. I was only 15, and I had my brother Jimmy, who was only 14 with me. Our mother and grandfather who had taken us to China three years ago were now gone. Our uncle had secretly gotten us out of China to Hong Kong. Now we were on our way back to America all alone. What would be awaiting us there?

My passport photo when I returned to America.

Where would we live? How would we survive? What kind of future would we have? Our uncle told me that one of our cousins would meet us in San Francisco when we arrived. We had no idea what to expect.

We left China in late January of 1951. The ocean voyage was very rough. From China to Japan the waves were so frightening. I was really in awe of what I was witnessing. The tremendous size of the ocean waves, as they seem to toss the huge ocean liner about like a toy ship. It seemed so strange as we would rise about three or four stories high and then drop about three or four stories down. It was hard to believe how small we were in comparison to the enormous size of the Pacific Ocean. At times, when we walked down the ship corridors we would literally have to walk with one foot on the floor and the other on the wall.

I remember watching a movie on a screen that was attached to the ceiling. As the ship was tossed around in the ocean, the movie screen swayed back and forth. I began to feel dizzy and quickly ran out of the door, barely making it to the handrail. I believe when I was finished being sick, the ocean had risen one more inch! In the dining room our chairs would slide back and forth and we'd have to hold on to our plates as we ate.

Leaving Japan on our way across the Pacific Ocean it seemed to be much calmer. As we left Japan I began thinking about our three years in China. I realized that we had experienced things

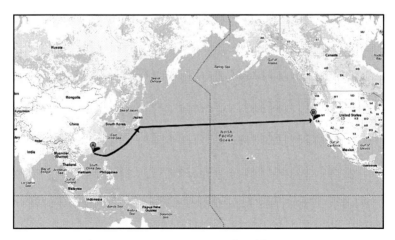

Our journey across the Pacific ocean

that we would have never known if we had not gone there. I was glad to have seen the differences in the culture, the living conditions, the language and many other aspects of life in this ancient country of my ancestors. Many things that we learned were customs that were centuries old, such as funeral rituals, wedding banquets, red egg celebrations and the giving of red envelopes, called "Lai See" that contained money for weddings, birthdays, New Year's and other special occasions.

Lai See - red envelopes for giving lucky money during special occasions.

At funerals, the Chinese passed out a piece of candy to everyone who came to give them "sweet" memories of the deceased which should be consumed that day before going home. They also gave out a small white envelope with a coin inside. White is the color reserved for death in the Chinese culture. Family and friends would also bring flowers and give the family white envelopes of money to help pay for the funeral. The family members would wear a black cloth band on their arm to show that they were in a period of mourning. If the deceased is a man, the band was worn on the left sleeve. If the deceased is a woman, the band is worn on the right sleeve. The mourning band was worn for the duration of the mourning period of one month. The immediate family members were not to visit other people's homes or other functions during the mourning period.

During the funeral, food, paper houses, imitation paper money and incenses were burned to ensure the loved one has a safe final journey and so they would have things in their after life. During the procession to the grave site, sometimes there would be "paid" grievers to convey the many friends the deceased one had if there were not many people able to attend. Food and incense would be placed at the grave annually during the cemetery clean up and visitation. Chinese customs dictate that all of the graves be honored if the relatives of the deceased could not be there because of distance or other reasons.

Weddings are also very special events in the Chinese culture. When a young man reached the age to marry, he would discuss it with his parents. They would make sure he was mature enough to handle the responsibilities that would be required of him. He must be able to support a family financially and emotionally. The parent would go to the other villages to announce that their son was ready for marriage. Parents with eligible daughters would contact the young man's parents and arrange a meeting with them in their village. A date would then be set for both families to meet. Sometimes there would be many families for the young man and his parents to visit. The perspective groom and his parents would visit each young woman and her parents to discuss things like the family's background, financial status, health issues, how much education each one had and the young man and woman's ideas about marriage. What is expected of each one of them? Could the woman cook, clean house, and do all of the things that is expected of a wife? Did she want children? Did the young man have good work ethics; is he responsible enough to do what is required of him as a husband? After visiting all of the families, the future groom and his parents would discuss which young woman would be the right one for him to marry. The young man and girl would meet alone to talk and get to know each other. More visits may be required before a final decision is made to approve the union of the son and daughter. Finally, the wedding date would be announced and all invitations would be carried to those that were invited. This would include all family members, relatives, friends and all of the important members of each village. All members of both families and many close friends would then be involved in the planning and preparation of the wedding banquet.

The families would decide on what dishes to serve at the wedding banquet. They would appoint someone to be in charge of the kitchen and the cooks. They planned the details of each dish to be cooked and the order that each dish would be served, as well as who would help clean up afterwards. They would choose hostesses to seat the wedding guests at their assigned tables. They would select men who would be servers to take each dish to the tables. They would also select a "Master of Ceremonies" who would be responsible for welcoming all the guest and introducing the wedding party: the bride and groom, the parents, brothers, sisters, relatives and all distinguished guests that were attending the wedding celebration banquet.

During the wedding ceremony the bride would wear the traditional red Chinese wedding dress. It was believed that the wedding dress should be red as it is considered the symbol of love and prosperity. It would be embroidered with gold or silver threads that included a dragon and phoenix. The dragon is the symbol of power. The dragon and phoenix together symbolizes the balance of male and female power.

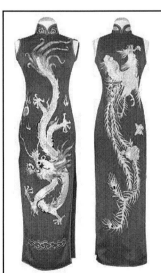

A traditional red wedding dress with ornate, gold, embroidery and sequins in the design of the Phoenix and the Dragon.

The wedding banquet feast would usually consist of seven or nine courses. The first course would be soup such as Bird's Nest soup. Following courses would be other traditional Chinese dishes, like plates of roasted pork, chicken, duck, shrimp with Chinese vegetables, abalone or squid with vegetables, black mushrooms with Chinese greens, whole steamed fish or mixed vegetable dishes, and of course, steamed white rice would be served.

Red Egg parties were given for newborn babies, usually after their first few months. Since the infant mortality rate in China was quite high, a baby reaching one month of age was likely to survive. So the new birth was then celebrated. This also gave the parents the opportunity to introduce their new baby to their friends and families. Eggs were boiled and dyed red and placed on each table to be eaten by family, friends and relatives. The egg is a symbol of fertility and the renewal of life and their round shape is associated with harmony and unity. The red color symbolizes happiness and good luck. An odd number of eggs represents a son has been born, while an even number of eggs means a daughter has been born. The baby is taken around the room of guests to be introduced and admired. Guests would bring gifts for the baby, which usually consisted of money if the baby was a boy, and gold and jade jewelry if the baby were a girl. Some babies are given tiger clothing. In Chinese folklore, the tiger is the king of beasts and it is believed to have special powers for protecting children. The money was presented in the traditional

Lai Cee red envelope, a symbol of wealth and success in the future. Traditionally, a boy's Red Egg party was more elaborate than a girl's, as the birth of a boy was valued more than the birth of a girl in the Chinese culture.

There were so many memories that I recalled as we sailed back to America. I would miss all of my relatives and all of the friends that we made in the village. But would I miss the slow pace of life, and the lack of conveniences that I had slowly become accustomed to? The uniformity of the clothing we wore. I would surely miss my aunt's cooking. I certainly would not miss the toilet pots, outdoor toilets, leeches and carrying poles of rice straw on my shoulders. I would definitely not miss the general lack of mobility between the neighboring villages! We had been in China approximately three years and during that time I can't recall ever going to any neighboring villages. I'm sure some people from neighboring villages must have come to some of the parties or banquets that occurred during this period, as our family was usually invited to attend most functions because our uncle was the Mayor of the village. He was often called upon to make special announcements or be the Master of Ceremonies. Surely other villagers were in attendance at these functions. Families with the same surnames started each of these villages. Some that I remember were the Wongs, Chins and Wings. Consequently, through the decades all residents of each village were related. You would have a village like ours where 80 to 90 percent would have the same surname Jeu. There were so many things I had learned about my family and my heritage that will remain with me forever. I hoped I could remember them and pass them on to my family some day.

We finally made it to San Francisco. We looked for our cousin but no one was there to meet us. We did not know him or know what he looked like. After about 30-45 minutes I was beginning to get worried. Jimmy was frightened and asked, "What are we going to do? We don't have any money." We spent our $5 on the ship. And all we had with us was a small suitcase with one change of clothes each. I looked in my pocket and found the paper my uncle had given me. It had our cousin's name, address and telephone number written on it. Harry Jeu, 1556 Stockton Street, San Francisco, California, Phone 2-8439. I saw a taxi and stopped him. Jimmy said, "What are you doing?" I told him that we had our cousin's address and we could get the taxi to take us there. When we arrived at our cousin's house he was surprised to see us. I told him that he would have to pay the taxi driver for us because we had no money. He never mentioned why he was not at the harbor, in fact, he did not seem too pleased to see us. It was a very awkward situation.

I finally decided to call Jimmy's teacher, Mrs. Gladys Walker and tell her where we were and what was going on. She had told us earlier in her letters, that if we ever left China and needed any help, to call her and she would help us. So after talking to her, she sent us some money through Western Union. It was enough to pay for two tickets to Memphis on the Greyhound Bus. After we stayed with our cousin for two or three days, we got on the bus and left San Francisco, heading back to Memphis. I remember our cousin gave us some bananas to eat on the trip but the bus driver told us that we could not take any fruit on the bus so we had to eat them before we left the bus station.

We finally arrived in Memphis with no money and only our small suitcase. Mrs. Walker had her employee Grant pick us up. The Walkers owned a Pure Oil Service Station on Hollywood Street in North Memphis. Gladys taught at Levi Elementary School in South Memphis where we had attended before going to China. Once we arrived in Memphis, I was planning to contact our cousin that we lived with while we were waiting on our Visas to be approved for the trip to China in 1946. I contacted our cousin, Mr. Jeu Chong and Mrs. Walker took us to his house. They had a grocery store on Walker Street in South Memphis. Back in those days the Chinese families would live in the rear or upstairs of their grocery stores. Mr. Chong was going to help us find someone to take us in or let us live with him until he could work out some type of solution for Jimmy and me. At that time, Mr. Chong had six children of his own. They had three boys and three girls, Frank, Richard, Davis, Frances, Peggy and Helen. Mrs. Walker suggested that Jimmy and I could go back home with her, since they did not have children and had room for us until we could decide what to do. So that is what we did. Eventually, the Walkers sat down with us to discuss our situation. Mrs. Walker asked us if we wanted to live with our cousins. I told her that I did, but I thought that since they had six children of their own, two more would be a burden for them. Even though they would have gladly taken us in, it was a similar situation we had just left in China with our uncle and his seven children.

Mr. and Mrs. Walker did not have children due to an injury Mr. Walker sustained while on duty in the military. During a paratrooper practice in North Carolina, Dallas jumped out of an airplane and his parachute did not open. He pulled the emergency parachute cord and it failed also. His life was spared when he fell through the roof of a barn and landed in the hayloft. He had many broken bones and injuries, which kept him in the hospital for over a year. Dallas was eventually medically discharged from active service due to the injuries.

Gladys said that we could live with them and work in their service station after school and on the weekends. We could attend Hollywood Jr. High School that was one block from their house. We called Mr. Chong to see what he thought about this solution. He said that if we both agreed to do this, we could try it for a while. He felt that he should take responsibility for us while we were back in America. But if things did not work out, we could come live with his family.

Now our journey living with Dallas and Gladys Walker began...

Jimmy, Gladys and me at Gladys' house that was next to the service station on Hollywood.

My Journey

Part 5
Living with Dallas and Gladys Walker

Dallas Walker

Gladys Walker

As we settled into our new home with Dallas and Gladys Walker we enrolled in the seventh grade at Hollywood Junior High School. I was 15 years old and Jimmy was 14 years old. We were the oldest students in the seventh grade since we had missed three years of school while we were living in China. The Walker's lived in a house that was next door to their service station. The backyard had a chain link fence with very thorny blackberry bushes planted in front to deter people from climbing over the fence. Jimmy would set an empty metal garbage can in the middle of the blackberry bushes to pick them and he would also be safe from any snakes on the ground. We would use

Walker's Pure Oil Service Station,
their house was next door on the left.

a sling blade to cut the tall grass around the back of the station. In the rear of the station were two large pecan trees. Gladys would always send pecans to her family in Virginia and Florida at Christmas time. There was a large covered concrete front porch about six-feet deep the full width of the house with a three-foot, metal glider sitting on the porch on the left side of the front door. There were boxwood hedges in front of the porch and on the south side of the porch was a narrow covered carport.

Jimmy and I converted a rear room of the house into our bedroom. I believe it had previously been a porch that had been crudely enclosed. We saw that the Walkers had a small house trailer in the back yard, the one that they had lived in when they first moved to Memphis. So after a few months of living on the back porch, we asked them if we could move into the trailer. Gladys said yes, if we really wanted to. So Jimmy and I cleared out the things that Gladys had stored in the trailer. We cleaned it up really well to make it livable and moved in. We had electricity for lights but no heat in the winter.

Our new home - the trailer in the Walker's back yard.

We would walk to Hollywood school every day, which was on Bryan Street, just behind our house. We adapted to the classes very easily and the English language came back to us very quickly. We met many new friends at Hollywood school. There was another Chinese boy going there, his name was John Chu. We found out that his family was from the village next to ours at the base of the mountain in China. We became very good friends with him.

John Chu's family, Mr. and Mrs. Fong Bong Chu, operated a grocery store at 2178 Chelsea Avenue and Hyde Park. They lived in the rear of the store, as most of the Chinese grocers did back then. I would

Jimmy and me in front of the trailer.

go there to visit with them sometimes. They were involved with the Lung Kong Tin Yee Association on Vance Avenue, the same one our grandfather would take us to. They would receive invitations to parties and John would invite us to go with his family. There were many parties there at that time; birthdays, red egg baby parties, weddings, new year's banquets and others similar to the parties we had in China. Most parties consisted of a meal of seven or nine delicious courses of home-cooked Chinese food similar to the food we had in China. At that time, each table would receive a fifth bottle of whiskey, which you could take home with you after the meal. If you paid your yearly dues of $30.00, you would always receive an invitation to all of the parties. We really enjoyed these celebrations. After graduation from Tech High School, John went to New York City and opened a restaurant there.

I became friends with many of my classmates at

Hollywood Junior High School. My best friend was Sterling Crutcher "Pat" Barr. We were in the same grade. Pat delivered the Memphis Press-Scimitar evening newspaper in a wagon that was pulled by his dog. He lived with his grandparents, Noble and Vernon Smith on Chelsea next to the drug store on the corner of Hollywood and Chelsea. Years ago this intersection was known as "Battle Block." There were two drug stores, a variety store and a furniture store. There was a bakery, Hollywood Theater and across the street, on the north side, was the Sterling Variety Store. On the northwest corner was Russell's Drug Store and next door, on Chelsea, was Billy Hubbard's Hardware.

Some of my other friends at Hollywood were Manuel Bell, Guy Smith, Jackie Berryhill, Billy "Red" Lindsey, Roby Nye, Tim Lemmon, Bobby Kitchens and David McDonald. Later, we all went to Tech High School. Most of them would come visit us after we got off work at the station.

There were many stores around the station on Hollywood. Vaughan's Furniture Store was next to the house on the north side, at the corner of Golden and Hollywood Street. Across the street from Vaughan's was a Corner Cafe. Next to the Cafe was a large parking lot for Hogue & Knott's Super Market. On the south side of the station was Home Lite Chain Saw Company. Across the street was a barbershop and a few houses. Further south down Hollywood, were the railroad tracks. I recall those railroad tracks became known at that time for drag racing between teen-aged hot rodders and the Policemen in "car 32," who would challenge all of the "hot rodders." If you could beat them across the tracks from the front of our service station (which was about 1/4 of a mile away) you were free to go. If you did not beat them, you belong to them! Car 32 was well known among the young teenagers in the community. If we hung out around the corner of the Drug Store, they would order us to go home.

We used to go to see movies at the Hollywood theater numerous times. I remember one time Jimmy and I took a large bag of popcorn to sneak into the theater, but Mr. Jim West, the owner, caught us and escorted us out, calling us "Little Communists." When we went to the Hollywood theater, we quickly learned always to come out after the movie was over in groups and never alone. If you came out alone, the policemen in car 32 were usually there waiting to harass you or worse, beat you with their nightsticks. They were always harassing the teenagers. You did not talk back to them, as they would hit you with their nightsticks. We learned to avoid them whenever we could. The police at that time were called "Crump's Cowboys." Mayor E. H. Crump was a very powerful influence in Memphis at that time.

Gladys and Dallas Walker were a very hard working couple. We began working with Mr. Walker in the Gas Station every day after school and on the weekends. They eventually laid off their only employee, Grant, after Jimmy and I had learned how to do his job. They said they could not afford to keep

Me, pumping gas at the Station.

him and pay us too. I really hated to see him leave. He had taught us so much and we really liked and respected him.

Every day, Gladys would come home from teaching school and cook dinner. Then she and Dallas would eat dinner while Jimmy and I ran the station. When they were through eating, they would come to the station and relieve us so we could go eat. After Dallas closed the station, Gladys would stay at the station and balance the day's receipts. She did this every day because the station was opened seven days a week.

On Sundays we would go to Sunday School at Hollywood Baptist Church, but did not attend services because Mrs. Walker wanted to have the station opened before church services were over. She wanted the church members to stop to buy gas for their cars on their way home. Sometimes Jimmy and I would skip Sunday School and go down the street to St. Mark's Methodist Church where my friend Jimmy Moore went. We would go to the Methodist Youth Fellowship to play ping pong with him.

Gladys Foley Walker was from Stuart, Virginia. The Foley's were a large family, she had a brother, Albert and six sisters: Bernice, Annis, Eunice, Agnes, Beatrice and Frances. Gladys received her teaching degree from William and Mary College in Virginia. After graduation, she met Dallas Wendell Walker. Dallas was from Pennsylvania. He was an Army Paratrooper and apparently was stationed in Virginia near where Gladys lived. Somehow they had met and eventually gotten married. Dallas wanted to go to an automotive school so he could open his own service station and there was a GMAC automotive school in Memphis, Tennessee on Summer Avenue. So he applied and was accepted. They moved to Memphis and bought a small trailer and moved into a trailer park on Summer Avenue. Gladys received a teaching position at Levi Elementary School in South Memphis. After Dallas finished automotive school and was certified, they bought the Pure Oil Service Station at 1334 North Hollywood Street, and the house next door. Gladys would drive the long daily trip from the service station in North Memphis to Levi School in South Memphis near the Mississippi State Line. It was about 15 miles each way.

Gladys grew up during the depression years so she was very frugal with their finances. She kept a very tight rein on all of the expenses of the Service Station. Sometimes, Dallas would do mechanical work on a customer's car and not log it in on the daily job sheet. He would put the money in his fishing tackle box to finance his fishing trips since Gladys would not give him much money for his trips. Jimmy and I would sometimes wash a car for 75¢ or fix a flat tire for 50¢ and not log it in the station journal so we would also have spending money. Once Mrs. Walker came home from school and checked the journal, and there was a big discrepancy in the money count. Dallas had forgotten to log in a large payment he had made for supplies. She called us all to come into the office and line up and turn our pockets inside out. This included Dallas too. When she discovered that Dallas had forgotten to log in the supply payment, she went to the house to cook supper. Dallas was

Gladys' graduation from Memphis State University, when receiving her Masters Degree in education.

really upset about this, he didn't say a word while we were being "searched and interrogated" but as soon as Gladys left, he made his usual remark, "Old battle ax - sees all, knows nothing!"

Gladys was so frugal, that she would only buy the food items that were advertised on sale in the grocery store ads. I recall Jimmy or I going with her from grocery store to grocery store all over town, just to buy all the items on sale. Dallas loved sardines, so when sardines were on sale, Gladys would always buy a whole case of them. We lived down the street from Hogue & Knot Super Market. Since we went there for every sale item, Hugh Hogue, the owner, became good friends with Gladys and Dallas. Hugh would allow Gladys to buy specials well above the advertised limits, which made her very happy.

While living with the Walker's, I recall that they never took vacations. The only holiday they would close the station for was Christmas. They never went to movies, concerts, parties or any events that I can remember. She had an obsession with saving money so she rarely spent any money to go anywhere. I recall her telling me that other children made fun of her because of her old clothes and shoes that she wore to school. They made remarks about her family being from the poor part of town. She had vowed that she would never be in that situation again. When she got home from school, she would change into some old dress and come out to the station to work until closing. She always wore old clothing when she worked at the station to give the impression that she could not afford finer clothes. And to give the impression that she did not have money to deter would-be robbers.

One time, one of her sisters called from Virginia and wanted to come see her to discuss some family business and stay with them for a visit. But Gladys told her we could meet them half way between Tennessee and Virginia at a roadside park that they agreed upon. She told Jimmy and me that we were going on a vacation. Boy, were we surprised! We left on Saturday after closing the station at 9:00 p.m. and drove all night to meet them at a park. We ate lunch, that we brought with us, visited with them for a while and then they took care of their business. We all got back into the car and drove all night to make it back to Memphis in time to open the station at 8:00 a.m. Monday morning. That was a vacation? It was the only one I remember taking with the Walkers.

Gladys and Dallas were total opposites. Gladys was the dominant one in the marriage. She was in total control of all their financial affairs. Gladys was always suspicious of people and had this fear that people would sue her if they could. She did not make friends easily and was not a very sociable person due to her suspicious nature. I remember one long time customer that had become very good friends with Dallas. He came by after work one day to buy gas and cash his payroll check. After he left to go home, Gladys called his wife and told her she had cashed his check and told her the amount so she could make sure he had that much with him when he got home.

Story of Two Brothers Who Fled From China to Memphis,
Printed in the Memphis Press-Scimitar, Dec. 1952.

When the husband found out what Gladys had done, he was infuriated. He came back to the station and confronted her about this and informed her he would never come back. He told her what she did was uncalled for and he was very upset. Afterwards he would only come by to see Dallas when Gladys was away or at school.

On the other hand, Dallas was a very outgoing person who made friends very easily. Everyone enjoyed being around him. Dallas had a very "salty" vocabulary and often "cussed like a sailor." All of the customers were accustomed to his rough language and seemed to overlook it. Dallas was always a very trustworthy person and sometimes customers would take advantage of him. Some customers became friends with him and would even go fishing with him on Saturday when Gladys would let him take a day off. Sometimes Jimmy would go with him. Dallas taught Jimmy how to fish and Jimmy really enjoyed it. Eventually, Jimmy became a better fisherman than Dallas.

Jimmy and I learned how to change oil, perform a grease job lubricate a car and fix a flat tire. We also learned to flush out the radiators, put in

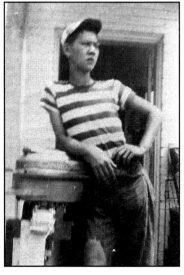

Me at the service station.

91

antifreeze and wash cars. We would pump gas, clean the windows, check the oil, water level and the air pressure in the tires of every customer's car. Jimmy was more mechanically inclined than I was. He learned how to adjust and install break shoes and would help Dallas with other mechanical jobs. Jimmy was really good at the mechanical work.

During that time, the Pure Oil Company would run an annual contest for all the stations in Memphis. The station that sold the most tires in a month would win a television set. Gladys told Jimmy and me that if we could help them win the contest that we could have the TV. So Jimmy and I worked really hard selling tires and we actually won the contest! The Pure Oil Company representative brought the television set to the station and presented it to us.

Me, in front of our trailer at the Walker's house when I was about 19 years old.

We were so excited and happy to have our very own television! Unfortunately, Gladys had other plans, she told us she was selling it to one of her customers, so we didn't get to keep it. Jimmy and I never tried to win any of the contests again. We did win more contests, but it was not because of us and Gladys always sold the prizes to one of our customers.

Gladys and Dallas paid Jimmy and me $15.00 a week for working at the gas station every day after school and on weekends. Gladys would deduct $10.00 for room and board. That left us with $5.00 for the week for spending money for movies (picture shows as they were called then) popcorn and drinks, clothing, hair products – shampoo and Brylcreem and anything else we may have needed.

After a while, Jimmy and I had saved up enough money for a down payment to buy a car. We bought our first car together, a 1952 Ford Coupe. Jimmy and I co-owned it and would alternate during the week and share it on the weekends. We decided we wanted to customize it, so we took it to Jimmy Saunders Body Shop on Summer Avenue which was known for customizing cars. They would remove the hood and trunk ornaments and the Ford nameplates. The holes were filled in with "Bondo," a mix that was used for repairing large dents and holes in cars. This was referred to as "leading in." We eventually decided on the color we wanted, a purple and light lavender color. I'm sorry, I do not have a colored photo of it, as we thought it turned out really nice (sharp – as guys in those days would describe their customized cars.) I eventually painted pinstripes on the hood, trunk and dashboard. Car dashboards at that time were painted metal and not padded like they are in today's cars.

Later, I bought my own car, a 1955 Chevy Convertible and I had it customized also. Jimmy Saunders painted it "Cobalt Blue." I told him I was going to pinstripe it myself. He asked me to bring the car by when I finished so he could see what I did. So later, after I had finished the pinstripes, I stopped by the shop to show him my work. Jimmy was very impressed and asked me if I would be interested in doing other cars. He said if I was, I could do some work in his shop on Saturdays and evenings. So I started going to his shop to pinstripe the cars that were there to be customized. This was certainly a stroke of luck; I could earn extra income doing something I really enjoyed.

I started going to the custom car shows at the Mid-South Fair Grounds on Sundays and my

My 1955 Chevy Convertible. It was Cobalt Blue. I did the custom pin striping myself.

reputation as a pin striper started getting around. People started paying me to pinstripe their cars at the shows. Sometimes people would come by the service station for me to paint on their cars. I would paint the cars for whatever the guys could afford with a $10.00 minimum. One of the most popular things at that time was a continuous pinstripe on the dashboards. I painted pinstripes on a lot of dashboards. It was also popular at that time to have a name painted on the front fender. I painted popular names such as "The Untouchables," "The Outlaws" and "Gang Busters." Or sometimes I would paint the owner's girlfriend's name. I eventually named my Chevy "Lil' Sherry" after our first daughter Sherry. I also painted flames on hoods and gas tank doors. I helped Pat Barr paint flames on his Studebaker. I continued painting pinstripes and custom names on cars through high school to earn extra spending money.

Sometimes we would "drag" Main Street. This meant driving up and down Main Street looking for girls. Of course we never met any girls doing that. I often wondered what we would have done if we had actually found some girls! We would go to Kay's drive-in on Crump Boulevard. Around the corner on Second Street was Gilley's drive-in restaurant. We never went there because it was the hangout of the Tiller brothers and their gang who had the reputation of being "wild." On the way home we would make stops at The Cotton Boll on East Parkway, Ray Gammon's and Porky's on Summer Avenue. This was a ritual with the teen aged boys with cars back in the 50's and 60's. We also went to the drive-in movie theaters. At that time, we had the Frayser drive-in, Summer drive-in, Bellevue drive-in and the Lamar drive-in. I remember one time going to the Sunset drive-in theater in West Memphis, Arkansas to see the movie "Mom and Dad." Billy Lindsey and another boy hid in the trunk of my car so they would not have to pay. The line was so long because everyone wanted to see this "risqué" movie. As we got to the ticket booth Billy yells out loud "are we in yet?" As we drove in and parked the guards came up as we opened the trunk and escorted us out. Needless to say, we did not get to see the movie that night.

One late night, Jimmy and I decided to sneak out and go for a joy ride. We picked up Jackie Berryhill and Billy Lindsey and wound up in Holly Springs, Mississippi. All of the sudden the car died and we couldn't get it started again. It was well after midnight but we had no choice, we had to call Dallas. We told him our problem and where we were. You do not want to know what actually he said! But after a while, he finally found us and worked with the car to get it running again. It was a low battery. Boy was he ticked off! He asked us why we were there and we told him we had gone out to get some coffee. Once again, you do not want to know what his reply was!

The principal at Tech was Mr. J.L. Highsaw. He was a very colorful and well-respected member of the Memphis educational system. I believe he was the first principal of Tech High when I arrived in

1954. During his later years Mr. Highsaw's eyesight had become a problem. He would roam the hallways by memory. He would enter the boy's restroom to try to catch students smoking. Eventually, as he entered the room everyone would stand still and be silent. He would look around the room and leave. Once during a pep rally in the auditorium, Mr. Highsaw was giving his annual dream speech of Tech defeating our high school nemesis Central. Normally, there would be a movable stair positioned in the front of the stage, but for some reason the stair unit was moved to the end of the stage. Mr. Highsaw finished his pep rally speech and walked to the center of the stage to step down as he had always done. The stage was at least three feet tall. Surprisingly, and to our horror, Mr. Highsaw fell off the stage and promptly stood up with both hands raised. The entire auditorium went wild! Tech very seldom beat Central at any sport.

Me sitting on Pat Barr's car at the service station.

Living with Dallas and Gladys was very unconventional as we began to find out. We did not live the way the families of our friends did. We did not have birthday party celebrations or cookouts. I recall Dallas had built a barbecue pit in the back yard, but we never used it while we lived with them. We never attended any community, church or school event. I am sure they were invited to social events from church members and friends. Why the Walkers never wanted to socialize with people was always puzzling to me. I believe Gladys was always afraid someone would criticize how she dressed, ate or acted. She once told us why she did not like to go out to eat at restaurants. While in college she went out to eat with some classmates. As they were eating, one of the classmates pointed out how Gladys was eating and they made fun of her. I never found out what it was that Gladys did that they were making fun of, but it was an event that stayed with Gladys throughout her life. Or was that just her way of not having to spend money eating out at a restaurant? I would say it was probably the latter.

Making ice cream with Gladys' nieces and a friend of ours, George Chandley. Jimmy standing on the left, me making the ice cream.

My Journey

Part 6
Schools After Returning to America

Upon our entering the seventh grade at Hollywood Jr. High School, we found it to be very comfortable, and all the teachers and students were very friendly to us. It was certainly different from the Chinese school in the village where one teacher taught five classes in a one-room building.

The school in China was dark and musty. I don't recall there being any windows in the school. There were small individual desks and wooden chairs. Our cousin, Jeu Mun Jip our uncle's oldest son had been our teacher. He would read from a book for the first grade class and assign them to study that lesson while he would instruct the next class. We would study the lessons assigned to us and would be required to recite them in front of the class the next day. He would continue this until all classes were assigned lessons. Each class, first through fifth grades were separated into small groups. After all the assignments were made to each class we would practice writing Chinese calligraphy on rice paper. We learned how to mix the black ink from an ink block with water to make the right consistency to write with. We would insert a sheet, with Chinese characters printed on it into a thin rice paper sleeve.

These sleeves were bound into a tablet. The paper was very transparent so you could easily see the printed characters that you were going to copy. After the last assignments we would have a study period. I had a difficult time getting adjusted to the way the Chinese students studied "out loud." It was very noisy and distracting for me.

As I walked into my seventh grade homeroom at Hollywood, Mrs. Bess Bourne, our homeroom teacher introduced me to my new American classmates. We had left America after completing the sixth grade, and after three years in China, we were placed in the seventh grade class. Jimmy and I were three years older than all of our classmates. I was wondering how I would be accepted as we started school. At the time, I thought Jimmy and I were the only Chinese students there, but we found out later that there was another Chinese boy there. His name was John Chu. He had a younger brother Howard and a younger sister Shirley who also attended Hollywood. Some of our classmates wondered if we could speak English. They did not know that we were born in Memphis and returned after living in China for three years. The English language came back to us very easily. I often wondered if we spoke correctly and if everyone could understand me. As time went by, we adapted to our new classmates and became very good friends with many of them.

The principal of Hollywood was Mr. Pete Callas. My Art teacher was Mrs. Tom Moss. I really enjoyed her art classes. Mrs. Moss encouraged me and guided me through many art projects. I will always remember the Christmas scene I helped paint on the second floor window above the school entrance on Bryan Street. My English teacher was Mrs. Jaffe. She was a very good teacher who would continuously push you. She was very demanding but I really enjoyed being in her class. Mr. Spray was the Coach and Woodwork's teacher. I believe basketball was the only sport we had. Coach Spray asked me if I would be interested in playing basketball. I was very excited and said I would like that. When I told Mrs. Walker about it she wanted to know more about what was involved in joining the team. I told her that I would have to practice after school and play at the other schools on Friday evenings. She said, "absolutely not!" I had to be at the station after school to help Dallas and Friday was one of the busiest days. Thus, ending my basketball career. I also joined the band but had to drop that too because of after school practices and events that would have taken me away from working at the service station after school.

Coach Spray was also my teacher in wood working class. I remember he taught us how to make a cedar chest. I still have that chest today. Even now, I still enjoy working with wood projects when I have the opportunity.

Miss Canada was the girl's Coach and Gym teacher. She was the youngest teacher there.

After leaving China, my sense of priorities were greatly changed. I understood the importance of a good education, a good work ethic, the value of money, friendship and honesty. I learned to associate with people who had good Christian values and I learned to always treat everyone equally no matter what nationality they were.

After graduating from Hollywood Jr. High in 1953, I joined many of my classmates and went to Memphis Technical High School on Poplar Avenue at North Claybrook. A few others went to Central High School. Jimmy and I often "hitch-hiked" to school just like most of the boys did in those days. Friendly people would pick us up as they drove down Poplar on their way to work downtown. They would drop us off in front of the school. Most of the time the same people would recognize us and luckily we would be

Tech High 1955

there when they drove by, so they would give us a ride again. Hitchhiking to school allowed us to save our bus fare for other things, which was usually the movies. One episode that I will always remember, was when a man stopped to give us a ride and I got in the middle and Jimmy sat by the window. As we proceeded down Poplar Avenue the man reached over and started stroking my left thigh. I immediately scooted over closer towards Jimmy and when we stopped at the next light, we bailed out of the car! After that, we only rode with people that we were familiar with who usually stopped to give us a ride.

I really enjoyed going to Tech. I adapted to the new school and new students immediately. There were so many activities to choose from. I begin to get involved in many activities such as the Key Club, Art Club, the Yellow Jacket High News Paper staff and the Tech Review Yearbook staff. I made many friends while at Tech. I was very involved in my art class and the yearbook staff where I did some of the artwork. I really enjoyed my Art classes taught by Mrs. Helen McGrath who gave

One of my watercolor paintings I won an award for in the Lowenstein's Art Contest.

Tech High 1954, Me and Jimmy

me much guidance and encouragement. This was one of my favorite classes. During my junior year we entered the Lowenstein's water-color contest and I won two awards for my paintings!

I even painted a Pure Oil can on the front brick wall at the service station for the Walkers. And every year at Christmas, I would paint a Christmas greeting and snow scene on the glass window in the front of the service station building.

I enjoyed the ROTC classes taught by M. Sargent Clarke Shaw. He and I became close friends. The "Key Club" sponsored by the Kiwanis Club was a boy's service group. In my senior year I was chosen as President. During that time I designed the Tech High car decal. The proceeds from this project were used towards the purchase of a new score board for the gym. Margaret Kelly was my homeroom teacher. She taught History classes. This was one of

Tech High 1955, Me and Jimmy

my favorite classes also. I had English under Gertrude Geraghty. She was a very interesting and entertaining teacher.

In my junior year, I got more

involved in school activities. I was nominated Boy's Vice-President and another Hollywood classmate, Jimmy Wendell Moore, was named Class

Tech High 1956, Me and Jimmy

President. He was Class President of all the classes that I was in from Hollywood to Tech. He was very popular and was involved in so many activities at Tech. He played football and basketball and was very good at both sports. He was liked by everyone. He and I had been good friends since Hollywood Jr. High. I was so envious of all the things that he was so capable of doing. Jimmy's ambition was to be a Methodist Minister. He eventually more than achieved that goal. He became the Minister of the largest Methodist Church in Houston, Texas and is the author of many best selling books.

They say that your High School experiences will be the happiest and most enjoyable times of your life, if you apply yourself. I certainly agree with that statement. These were the days of duck tail hairdos, T-shirts with cigarettes rolled up in the sleeve, Levis with rolled up pant legs, Penny loafers, Argyle socks, bobbie socks, 45 and 33-1/3 vinyl records. Black and white TVs with Amos and Andy, Fibbe McGee and Molly, the Shadow, the Lone Ranger, Roy Rogers, Gang Busters, Gun Smoke, the Ed Sullivan Show and the Dinah Shore's Chevrolet Theater just to name a few. I thoroughly enjoyed being at Tech. Making new friends, attending some remarkable classes and participating in the many activities that were offered. My high school years were so rewarding to me.

I have many life long friends that were classmates of mine at Hollywood Jr. High and Tech High School that I have remained in touch with after all of these years. Pat Barr, my best friend from Hollywood and Tech., Wanda and her sister Frances (Billie) Martin. We see each other at our Tech dinners at Piccadilly Restaurant on Mt. Moriah. Wanda told me she still has the picture I drew of her in art class at Tech. Jerry "Ronnie" Bryant was a close friend at Tech also. There are the Hollywood and Tech buddies – Tim Lemmon, Jackie Berryhill, Guy Smith, my ROTC sponsor Virginia Bell, Seth "Tommy" French, Rose Marie Kane, Mary Lee King, Bobby Kitchens, Earlene Mayo, Barbara Seagraves (who later married my best friend Pat Barr), Martin Willis and many others.

On December 20, 1955 I was invited by Pat Barr to accompany him on a double date to Frayser High School's Girl's Athletic Club Christmas Party. We were to pick up his date Sue Simpson and we would meet my "blind date," Elizabeth "Libby" Hannis, at the party because she was one of the students helping set up and decorate. As we got to the school parking lot, Pat let Sue out of the car to get Libby to come out to meet us. We moved the car to a parking spot near the door to the gymnasium where the Christmas party was being held. While we were waiting, I told Pat that I have never been on a "blind date" and I wished I had never agreed to do this. In the 1950's segregation was in effect & prejudice was the norm. I was always afraid to ask girls out for a date because I didn't know how her parents would react when they found out I was Chinese. I asked Pat, "Have you ever met this girl?" He said "No." Boy, I was thinking, this had better turn out good or I will make him pay dearly. Sue finally came out with Libby following her, I had never had the experience that I felt at that moment, when I saw this beautiful girl with Sue. I was so dazed that I could not think straight. When Sue introduced us I stammered out my name. As we went into the gym, Libby wanted me to meet her gym teacher, Miss Frances Hoback. As we approached Miss Hoback, she saw me and said, "George, what are you doing here?" I said that Pat had forced me to come with him or he would not have been able to come. (Boy was I glad I came!) Frances Hoback was from the Hollywood Community. She knew Pat also. Pat and I were classmates with her brother Jack Hoback who ran around with us. Libby and Sue were really surprised that we knew their teacher. As we were talking with Frances, Libby asked me if I wanted some hot chocolate and I said yes. Then she asked if I wanted marshmallows in it. Still in a confused state, I stammered out "no thanks, I don't put mushrooms in my hot chocolate." Boy, how stupid was that? Libby probably thought that I didn't know the difference between a marshmallow and a mushroom! Talk about starting off on the wrong foot! Was I embarrassed! Libby asked me to dance and I told her I wasn't much of a dancer, so she asked if I minded if she danced with other boys. A lot of boys kept coming over to ask her to dance. That's when she told me that she was a member of the Frayser High's dance team. They attended "Wink Martindale's Dance Party" that was on television on Saturdays. After the dance we went to Kay's drive in on Crump Blvd, where Sue's dad worked. He gave all of us a barbecue sandwich and a drink.

Sue had to be home at 11:00 p.m. so we had to leave to take her and Libby home. On the way back home Pat asked me if I didn't want to see Libby again would I mind if he asked her out for a date. I told him I liked her and he could NOT ask her out for a date unless she did not want to go out with me again. Christmas week was a busy time at the station so I didn't get to call Libby until after Christmas. I also didn't have any money as it was spent on gifts for Jimmy, Dallas and Gladys and other friends. I couldn't ask Libby out for a date until after the holidays when I got my next paycheck. I finally did get to call Libby and we saw each other on the weekends.

As we continued to date, Libby and I became closer. She was very easy to talk to and she was very mature. We would spend hours talking about our future. I was so convinced that this girl was the one I wanted to spend the rest of my life with. I knew that she would be a good wife, mother and friend. As we continued to see each other I wondered if Libby would continue to see me. Was there to be a future for us? I certainly wanted to be with her.

George and Libby

For Libby's initial introduction to Chinese food, I took her to Joy Young's Chinese Restaurant, at Third and Union Avenue near downtown Memphis. I was very nervous about what to order. I wanted her to enjoy this dinner. I don't remember all that I ordered, but one dish was stir-fried Chinese barbecued pork with bean sprouts, one of my favorites. I noticed Libby was picking at her dish. She was pushing all of the bean sprouts aside. She later told me when they grew beans in the country and the beans started sprouting, you did not eat them, you'd throw them away. But I think that she enjoyed her new

Juanita playing our records

experience. That dish, char siu bean sprouts, soon became one of her favorite dishes.

As time went by, we would talk every night, sometimes for hours. Some Fridays she would stay after school for something she was involved in and I would pick her up at Frayser High School. Then we would go to her house. They lived on Oxford Drive near Overton Crossing. It was a small house on a wooded lot. She kept my 45-RPM record player at her house so I would not have to bring it back and forth when I came to visit her on the weekends. We would have our own dance party. Some weekends her Aunt Frances and cousin Faye would come from Middleton, TN and join us. We would have a great time. Libby's mom Juanita (Neda) would make popcorn and other snacks for us. Libby's sister, Carlene would invite some of her friends to join us. Neda enjoyed it as much as we did. She was our D.J. and kept loading up records on my record player, always playing the good old songs such as Fats Domino singing "Blueberry Hill", that was always the first song Neda would play, as he was her favorite artist. We also loved to dance to Elvis, The Platters, Jerry Lee Lewis, Roy Orbison and The Everly Brothers. There were others that were always played too. We would stay up late Saturday night and have a good time dancing.

Libby's dad, Jack Hannis, was working for International Harvester and was being transferred to Jackson, MS. When they moved away I thought we would never see each other again. I could not call her as often as I had been doing, as it would be long distance charges and would cost too much, so we started writing to each other. She kept me informed about all she was doing and her experience of having to go to two schools to be able to take Latin as she did at Frayser High. Jimmy and I drove to Jackson once to see her. Later she wrote and told me they were moving back to Memphis. I was so happy I could not believe it. I had missed her so much, now we would continue seeing each other. My prayers were answered.

That year I wanted to give Libby something really special for Christmas, so I bought her a mouton jacket. She was so surprised when she saw it. She still has it today after all these years! The senior prom was coming up soon. It was to be at the Skyway in the Peabody Hotel, in downtown Memphis. We were going with Libby's best friend, June Tinsley and a friend of mine George Kisner, who had been a classmate of mine from Hollywood Jr. High and Tech High School. We went in my car. Libby wore this beautiful dress and looked so gorgeous in it. We really had a wonderful time.

Prom Photo & Program 1956

Libby on the left, with a friend, Libby's sister Carlene and Barbara Seagraves (my best friend Pat's, girlfriend)

On the weekends I would pick up Libby and her sister Carlene, who had to "chaperone" us and we'd go to Overton Park, Shelby Forest or Riverside Park. Sometimes Pat Barr or Jackie Berryhill would go with us. Sometimes we would have a picnic, but most of the time we would clean and wax our cars. I had a portable record player then, that you would crank with a handle. You would lift the heavy headpiece and insert a needle onto a 78 or 33-1/3 vinyl record. We would turn the volume up as loud as we could. We would really have some fun times riding around with my old record player! Our favorite song was "Band of Gold" by Don Cherry. Some of the other songs we liked were the Platters "The Great Pretender" and "Harbor Lights," "Wake Up Little Susie" by the Everly Brothers and "Love me Tender" by Elvis. There were many others we enjoyed listening to. The music of the 50's and 60's were and still are, some of my favorite songs. We really had some enjoyable times.

One time we were picnicking at River side Park with Neda, Carlene and some other friends and while we were waxing my car and giving my record player a wind every so often to play our records, a family picnicking next to us heard the music and came over to see where the music was coming from. They were amazed, they had never seen or heard of such a thing as a record player. I still have that 45-RPM record player today; it even has some spare "needles" left in the little storage compartment too!

My old wind-up 45 rpm record player.

I remember Jimmy, Jackie Berryhill, Bill (Red) Lindsey and I decided to do something really daring one night. We decided we'd walk through Overton Park forest at midnight, not using the pathways or any flashlights, and trek through it to the other side. That was a scary adventure that I will always remember. What dumb, but fun things we did in our youth! We should be thankful that we survived some of the more dangerous feats that our young minds thought of doing.

George and Libby's high school photos

Jackie Berryhill (right) on the hood of his '49 Ford and me (left) on the hood of my '55 Chevy. This picture was taken in front of the "Dough Boy" statue in Overton Park.

Other School Memories
Photos from my Tech High yearbooks

R.O.T.C Color Guards, 1955
That's me on the left and my best friend Pat Barr
second from the right.

Lowenstein's Water Color Contest Winners, 1955.

Art Club, 1955

Junior Class Officers and Their Director, 1955
*Front row, left to right: Elvis Anderton - Sergeant-at-Arms;
Jimmy Moore - President; Nancy Evans - Reporter. Second row: Shirley Mason - Girls' Vice President; Starlon
Moorman - Secretary; George Jeu - Boys' Vice President.
Third row: Pat Burkes - Treasurer; Junell Kelso - Chaplain.
Standing: Coach James Sivert.*

Key Club Hopes To
Buy Scoreboard

A big project of the Key Club
the sale of Tech Decals. The design,
blue and gold, a Yellowjacket
around a large T, was de...

Key Club, 1955.
That's me, second row, second from the right. President.

Members of the Hall of Fame, 1955

Left to right: Friendliest - Shirley Gentry and George Jeu; Cutest - Dot Taylor and Elvis Anderton; Best-all-around - Shirley Mason and Starlon Moorman; Best Dressed - Irma Phifer and Don Roach; Wittiest - Claudia Riddle and Guy Smith.

Art Club, 1956

Decorating the gym for the art club dance. Gerald, Ann, George, Jack, Cecile, Sonia, Jo Ann and Billy.

Key Club, 1956

Discussing the sale of decals to raise money for the Key Club. Officers, seated: Jimmy Moore, Phil Wright, George Jeu, Lewis Willis. Standing: Larry Harrison and Mike Lindsey.

Annual Staff, 1956

Studying a layout problem are some of the staff editors, George Jeu, Nancy Ellis, Pat Brandon and Barbara Tanner.

Most Intellectual, 1956
George Jeu and Pat Ragan

National Honor Society 1956
Barbara Tanner - President, Nancy Ellis - Vice President, Billy Paris
- Secretary, Vernean Drake - Treasurer, Pat Brandon - Chaplain, Jim-
my Moore - Parliamentarian, Barbara McDade - Sgt-at-Arms, Pat
Burkes - Reporter, Members: Sue Brassell, Doris Caldwell, Elaine Cobb,
Bertha Doyle, Mary Ann Gallarno, Shirley Gentry, Juanita Holloway,
George Jeu, Jimmy Langford, Barbara Lyle, Mary Lou Mask, Patricia
Meals, Pat Ragan, Wanda Roberts, Janet Stroud, Donna Tate, Joan
Willis, Martin Willis and Bobby Griffin. Sponsors: Louise Clark, Harry
Esslinger and Margaret Kelly.

*An article printed
in the Memphis
Press-Scimitar
in 1955 or 1956.*

Young Memphis

George Jeu

Flair For Color And Line
Is This Student's Gift

GEORGE JEU is a shy young man with a deft pencil and brush. This American-born Chinese, a senior at Tech High School, seems to have the Oriental flair for art.

Proof of George's talent is the capture of two key awards in the Lowenstein-sponsored art competition for Mid-South boys and girls. He belongs to Tech High's Art Club and is staff artist for the school annual, "Tech Review."

Posters, too, are his talent, and George can be found preparing one for some event almost any week. Just now he's engaged in making political posters for the school election.

At 20 George is still in high school due to a break in his American education at the time his parents returned to China to live. His ailing mother chose to return to her homeland, where she died, her husband succeeding her in death. George and his brother, Jimmy, one year younger, were left in the care of their uncle there.

While in China the boys attended Chinese schools, a difficult ordeal in view of their ignorance of the language.

"I failed the first grade," was George's expressive comment.

Through the efforts of their uncle, George and Jimmy returned to America under the guardianship of Mr. and Mrs. Dallas Walker of 1338 Hollywood, with whom they are now living. Both the boys are Tech High seniors.

Although Chinese schools were difficult, George has done above-average work in his own American schools. He is a member of the Honor Society and is described by one teacher as "a good all-around student."

George is a member of Sportsman Club and Key Club and is on the staff of "Yellow Jackets," school paper. In addition, he works as a gas station attendant after school hours.

With his artistic bent, naturally George aspires to a future in art and, given a scholarship, hopes to prepare himself for a commercial art career.

—RUTH JACQUEMIN

My Journey

Part 7
My First Job

After graduating from Tech in May of 1956, I wondered what lay ahead for me. I was looking for a summer job before starting school at Memphis State. My former R.O.T.C instructor, Clark Shaw called me one day and said that he had a job for me if I was interested. He had retired from Tech in my Junior year and began working for Continental Baking Company (Wonder Bread) as supervisor of the special events department. He told me that the Wonder Bread route men would secure sign requests from the local and rural grocery stores in Tennessee, Arkansas and Mississippi. The job included installing two 4" x 4" x 8' wood posts with the stores name on a 1' x 4' long metal panel and a 3' x 4' metal Wonder Bread panel below. We would apply store name decals to the front windows and Wonder Bread decals to the

---

bottom of the windows. This job sounded interesting to me. Sgt. Shaw told me I would be paid $50.00 a week with full benefits. I told Sgt. Shaw I would be interested in working through the summer before I started at Memphis State and I was hired. This began my real job experience after graduating from Tech.

I really enjoyed my job at Wonder Bread. We would load up with the Wonder Bread panels, the blank name panels and the posts. Then we would load up our tools – post-hole diggers, nails, hammers and other equipment into an old green panel truck. We usually serviced all the work orders in each state. We would service all grocery stores in the Memphis area which usually consisted of the store name on the front window and Wonder Bread decals at the bottom. Originally, we used decals on the name panels and windows, then one day I suggested to Sgt. Shaw to let me try hand painting the name panels. He agreed, so we bought lettering brushes, paint, mineral spirits for cleaning the brushes and other related supplies that I would need. I eventually became effective at hand lettering the signs. We discontinued using decals and eventually I started painting on the sides of the exterior wood siding or brick walls of grocery stores. We would paint the store name in large letters and I would paint a large loaf of Wonder Bread below. Competition among the bread companies was fierce at that time. The position of the bread shelf unit was very sought after. Each route man would offer many free services to secure the best shelf locations. Usually that would be the end of the shelf as the customer entered the store. Some route men would offer store owners services like building more shelves, repairing some areas inside the store, painting the outside of the building and things like that. We traveled to many small towns throughout the Mid-South – Millington, Brunswick, Covington, Somerville, Bartlett, Mason and others in Tennessee. In Arkansas we traveled to West Memphis, Marion, Hughes, Earle, Parkin, Marked Tree, Lepanto, Wilson, Forrest City and others. Mississippi towns included Southaven, Horn Lake, Olive Branch, Hernando, Holly Springs, Tunica, Como and others.

I thoroughly enjoyed traveling to these rural towns to paint their store windows and walls. In the small rural town grocery stores I would meet many Chinese store owners who would ask me who my parents were. When I told them, they would tell me they knew my parents and some of them would tell me we were relatives and were from the same village in China. I will always remember the many rural Chinese Grocery Stores that we serviced, such as the Young's in Earle, AR, the Lock's in Hughes, AR, the Wah's in Turrell, AR (Charlie Wah became the first Chinese Mayor in the Mid-South), the Fong's in Hughes, AR and the Lum's in West Memphis, AR. Since many of these Chinese grocers had known my parents and my grandfather, I soon established friendships with them. All of them would always offer me a soft drink and something to eat while I was there. This is a typical Chinese custom when a cousin or friend visits you. Sometimes I would get to eat some really good Chinese food like my Aunt used to cook for us in China.

I continued working for Wonder Bread throughout the summer, but I was looking forward to attending Memphis State University in September. As the business grew, we started servicing more grocery stores, so we had to hire another employee to assist us. I remembered a friend of mine that had been looking for a job, without success. We had been classmates at both Hollywood and Tech High. His name was Jackie Berryhill. I called him and he said he would be interested in the job. Jackie came in and interviewed for the position and was hired immediately. He started the next day. Years later, we continued on our separate career paths, for other sign shops and eventually he had his own sign shop, "Berryhill's Signs."

One thing I will always remember from all the trips to Arkansas to install the road signs for the grocery stores. We had to dig two post holes, three feet deep to secure the signs to. I learned that the dirt in Arkansas was known as "gumbo." When you dug down with the post hole digger, it went down pretty easily, but when you tried to bring it back up it was really hard. The ground seemed to stick to the post hole digger which made it very difficult to pull out of the ground. This made installing road signs in Arkansas really hard work! The road signs were much easier to install in Mississippi and Tennessee.

I remember one rural grocery store in East

Tennessee named Joe's Grocery. He wanted us to paint on the side of the building "Git Mo Fo Yo Do At Jo's Sto." How strange was that? Would people really understand what it said or meant? Can you?

While working at Wonder Bread, I also learned how to paint letters in reverse on the inside of the store windows. This prevented the letters from being exposed to the outdoor elements and made the lettering last longer.

Once we were painting on a large billboard on top of a grocery store at South Third Street in South Memphis. I was on the top rungs of a long extension ladder, hand lettering the store name on a billboard. Suddenly, I felt a slight movement in the ladder. Then I noticed two streak marks on the billboard made by the ladder, indicating that the ladder (with me on it) was sliding down. I yelled at Jackie to come and hold my ladder as I slowly slid down the face of the billboard.

Another time, on a very hot day, we were working on a tar roof. As it got hotter, the tar got softer and the base of the ladder slowly began to slide. It was so slow that I did not notice the ladder was moving while I was lettering on the top of the billboard. Jackie held the ladder as I slowly climbed down. That could have been a disaster for me. The summer went by very quickly, and as the days went by, I looked forward to starting school at Memphis State.

I remember going to Lake Cormorant, Mississippi to our cousin's grocery store to put signs on their windows. Since we were there in the morning she wanted to cook breakfast for us. When we finished the signs Mrs. Tong invited us to the kitchen in the rear of the store. As I sat down at the table she put a plate of bacon and a plate of eggs on the table. I waited on George and Roosevelt to sit down but she told me to go ahead and eat as those two plates of food were for me. One plate had one pound of bacon and the other had six eggs. I told Mrs. Tong that I could not possibly eat this much. She told me that's what she always cooked for her sons. I was doing good to eat four pieces of bacon and two eggs! Her sons, George and Roosevelt (everyone called him "Rose") were football players with very hardy appetites!

At some of the other rural Chinese grocery stores we would get pickled pigs feet, pickled eggs, pickled sausage, hoop cheese, crackers, Cokes, R.C. Colas, NuGrape or other drinks. One of my favorite drinks was the Chocolate Soldier.

My Journey

Part 8
Life Lessons Learned

While growing up, as a teenager you unknowingly inherit life lessons during the every day things that you encounter. These lessons begin to mold you into the person that you will become as an adult. Although, at times it is hard to believe that some of these lessons will serve you well throughout your life. I believe my most important lessons in my life began while I was living with Gladys and Dallas Walker, our foster parents. They helped me build a foundation that I have lived by all of my life.

When we agreed to live with the Walkers, they informed us what we were to do in return for them. We would work in the Service Station with Dallas after school; do household chores such as sweeping and mopping the linoleum floors in the kitchen, hallway and back laundry room. We would wash clothes in the wringer washer, rinse them in the two-compartment rinse tub and hang the clothes out on the clothesline in the back yard to dry. We would mow the yard in the summer with their rotary blade push mower. These chores would be alternated between Jimmy and me on the weekends. This life lesson instilled in me throughout my teen years, was the value of how important it is to have a good work ethic. The Walkers taught me how to do these tasks and also taught me why it was important to do them on a timely routine schedule.

After closing hours at the Service Station, we were expected to do our school homework. This was every night or as needed before we could do anything that we wanted to do, such as reading comic books, building model cars and airplanes and in my case, drawing. We could not have friends over until our studying was done. This life lesson taught me how to prioritize my time, and how important it was to schedule my time wisely.

I learned a lot of what I consider to be very important to me through watching Gladys and Dallas in their daily lives. Even though Gladys had a strange personality, I began to understand the childhood that she encountered as she was growing up in the poor section of Virginia. I always suspected there were many things in her life that she kept suppressed. I soon learned that outwardly, she seemed suspicious of everyone, and it was hard for her to openly express her true feelings. But in spite of all that Gladys had gone through, and her poor childhood, she always helped those who were in need and was supportive of those who were "looked down upon" by others. From this I learned not to judge people by their appearance and to treat everyone equally.

Gladys taught us the importance of saving money by helping us start a savings account at the bank. She also helped us obtain an accidental Life Insurance policy with Life and Casualty Insurance Company for .10¢ a week. She would not let us buy our first car until we were able to make the monthly payments and insurance payments. We were to have enough to pay for gasoline also. We learned how to budget our finances very carefully thanks to Gladys.

Dallas very seldom talked about his family. We knew that he had two sisters; Peggy and Betty and two brothers; Wendy and Clarence who had died early in life. Dallas grew up in Pennsylvania. He was an Army Paratrooper when he met Gladys. Dallas was a very outgoing person with a very jovial personality. He enjoyed being around people and once people got to know him they eventually became good friends. He was very easy to talk to, even though he had this very gruff facade on the outside, he was really a very mischievous "teddy bear" on the inside. Dallas never worried about what people thought about him. He always treated everyone the same. Dallas loved to tell jokes. I remember some of his customers would stop to get gas or other services and stay to visit with Dallas afterwards. The life lesson I learned from Dallas through his friendliness was to always be yourself. Be friendly to everyone and accept people as they are.

One life lesson that I learned while living and observing how the Walkers related to the customers that they served was that the customer always came first. The neighborhood we lived in was basically a mixture of whites and blacks around us, so we had many black customers. Some of the black men became good friends with Dallas and would often stop by after work to visit with him. One of Dallas' customers was a man named Joe Benson. He and Dallas became best friends. Joe would often stop by after work and visit with Dallas. Some weekends Joe would come by and help Dallas with some of the auto work. Joe and Dallas often went fishing together. Joe took Jimmy and me under his wings and was very protective of us. He was a very large man and a very friendly person. Jimmy and I both became very fond of him. Other customers would also go fishing with Dallas on weekends when Gladys, Jimmy and I could take care of the station. In those days in Memphis, it was uncommon for whites and blacks to mix sociably, but Gladys and Dallas grew up in areas where there were few blacks. Gladys grew up in the Virginia Hills and Dallas in Pennsylvania. They did not have the racial prejudice that was so prevalent in the south during that time. These observations were instilled in both Jimmy and me through the way the Walkers treated all of their customers. We had two restrooms at the station, one on the inside labeled "white" and one on the outside of the station labeled "colored". Blacks were not allowed to use the same facilities as the whites at that time, if they did, they could be arrested. I remember sometimes if the colored facility was occupied, Dallas would tell the black customers to go ahead and use the white one. Some of them would and some of them would not. I believe this is one of the most important life lessons that I inherited from Gladys and Dallas. Do not judge people by the color of their skin.

It's amazing how my priorities changed living in America, after having lived in China for three years. Things that we had always taken for granted, were now very appreciated. Electricity – lights in every room operated by a light switch on the wall. It took me a while to stop saying, "blow out the lights." Outlets to plug in radios and other electrical appliances, refrigerators with ice and toasters. Indoor plumbing – toilets, kitchen sinks and washing machines. Transportation – the ability to travel long distances by car, bus, train or airplanes. A Safe and Clean Environment – local Fire and Police protection, garbage trucks with people who would pick up your trash and take it away. Did you know that back in those days Memphis was named the cleanest city in the nation for many years? Food – the availability of good foods from local grocery stores. Entertainment – movie theaters, televisions, stock car racing in West Memphis, Memphis Chicks ball games with the "Chickasaw Buddies" Fan Club at Russwood Ball Park on Madison Avenue, picnics and games at Shelby Forrest State Park and Overton Park. The Zoo in Overton Park. Education – the luxury that everyone could go to school without having to pay. Shopping – the wide variety of shopping available downtown – Goldsmith's Department Store, Lowensteins, Brys, Kress 5 & 10, Black and White Clothing Store, Walgreens Drugs, The Planters Peanut Store where the mechanical peanut man was riding the peanut roaster and tapping on the window. And the smell of fresh roasting peanuts was being blown outside to entice everyone to come in. Restaurants – Krystal burgers on Summer Avenue at National, where the girls delivered your order on roller skates, those huge Lot-O-Burgers on Thomas, Porky's and Leonard's barbecue sandwiches, fried shrimp at Anderton's Seafood Restaurant downtown, lobster Cantonese at Joy Young's Chinese Restaurant at Third and Union Avenue and hot tamales and Mexican cheese burgers from Pancho's in West Memphis. The Cotton Boll Drive-in on East Parkway across from Overton Park and Kay's Drive-in on Crump Blvd.

I can't image what could have happened to Jimmy and me, left all alone on that dock in San Francisco. What if the Walkers had not been so willing to help us? I've faced so many turning points in my life and the experiences I've lived through strengthened me and guided me to live on. All that I've endured has made me thankful for all of the blessings I've been given, all the friends that I have made through the years and especially all of my relatives who helped Jimmy and me in our life without parents. It is our past that helps us become men and our experiences that make us who we are today.

Libby and I eventually married and had three beautiful daughters Sherland (Sherry) Ann, Kerri Faye and Anita Kay. Now Libby and I are on another fantastic journey, with our daughters as a family.

*Me, Libby,
Sherry
and Kerri*

*I always kept
my promise to
my mother and
made yearly
trips with Libby
and the girls to
Little Rock to
visit my dad's
grave site.*

My hopes for the future are that the life that I have lived will be remembered. That as a husband to Libby for 50 plus years, I gave her the love and devotion that she so much deserved. That I was what she wanted in a husband and father to our daughters – Sherry, Kerri and Anita. She is the wife, friend and lover that I had always dreamed of having. I thank God for giving me such a precious gift.

To my daughters I wish that they will remember me as a father who so dearly loved them and always tried to teach them the things that would guide them as they grew into adulthood. I pray that they will always cherish the times that we shared together on those special adventures on our journey as a family.

To my grandchildren I hope their future is full of great and fulfilling promises as they approach adulthood. May they always aspire to achieve their goals, follow their dreams and live their lives full of love of God, love of life, love of family and love of service. I hope they will strive to make the right decisions as they work towards the goals for their future. And that they will remember the times we've shared and the things I taught them.

GEORGE JEU

Family dinner at our house. (left to right) Dallas, Jimmy, me, Gladys and Libby.

Dallas and me in the kitchen.

Trip to Washington, DC with Dallas.

My first job as an Architural Draftsman at George A. Thomason's office

Jimmy, Mae, Gladys, Libby and me.

George's 70th birthday with Libby and the girls.

Christmas 2011 - Back: Blaine, Sharon, Jeremy, Kerri, Carlene, Sherry, Anita, Libby, Wesley, Ron. Sitting: Frances, Jeanette, George, Jimmy, Mae. Front: Kaitlyn, Natalie, Lilly.

George and Libby with the grandchildren.
Back: Jeremy, Natalie, Will, Joel, George;
Front: Lilly, Libby, George, Kaitlyn.

The second printing of this book is dedicated to the memory of my loving husband and father George Jeu.

His battle with cancer was finally over on April 4, 2014, but his memory and spirit will live in our hearts until we meet again.